Date Due

NOV 12 '69			

MUSIC AND PEOPLE

•

MUSIC
AND
PEOPLE

·

NED ROREM

GEORGE BRAZILLER · New York

94177

Dedicated with love to
Maggy von Magerstadt-Fisher
James Roland Holmes
Thomas Prentiss
David Diamond
Rosemarie Beck and Robert Phelps
and as always to my faithful parents
Gladys Winifred Miller and Clarence Rufus Rorem

Contents

•

Preface

•

. . . criticism has two different aspects: one is being made drunk for a second time by seeing something happen; the other is expressing lucidly what you saw when you were drunk.
—EDWIN DENBY,
Dancers, Buildings and People in the Streets

THIS COLLECTION PURPOSES TWO ATTITUDES OF one person toward the artistic (mostly musical) tone of the fairly recent past and of the present. The first attitude, presumably objective, is embodied in a series of articles and reviews dealing with personalities or trends. These are interspersed with Interludes, unquestionably subjective, derived from my diary: random notes, sometimes forming postscripts to the essays, more often taking their own disordered path. That path is the problematic one of the artist today, particularly the artist who is myself.

Certain thoughts overlap within these pages. *Tant pis!* Rather than editing out repetitions I've opted for non-revision, less from laziness than for reinforcement: the same idea reiterated in a different context both alters emphasis and re-echoes what was in the air—at least in my air—during the sixties.

None of the Interludes has been previously printed. Some of the "set pieces," in somewhat changed versions, first appeared elsewhere as follows: "The Beatles" in *The New York Review of Books*; "Bernac and Poulenc" in *High Fidelity*; "Richard Strauss" and "Twentieth Century Music" in *The New York Times Book Review*; "Makers of Manners" in *Vogue*; "Foss Improvises" in *Musical America*; "Flanagan" in *American Composers Alliance Bulletin*; "Toscanini" and "Where Is Our Music Going?" in *The American Record Guide*; "Last Thoughts On The Beatles" in *The Village Voice*. "Ezra Pound as Musician," written as a preface to Plenum Press's reprint of a treatise by Pound, was first published in *The London Magazine*, then in *The American Record Guide*.

All of these appeared in the past year, with the exception of "Flanagan," which dates back to 1960, and "Foss Improvises," written in 1961.

Finally, "I'd Take The Fire" has undergone various mutations. The "nucleus" describing that first visit to Cocteau in 1951 was extracted from my diary and enlarged into an "Epitaph" published in *The Village Voice* in 1963. It was enlarged still more for *The Paris Diary* in 1966. In 1967 it was revamped as a *précis des oeuvres* to serve as Introduction for *The Difficulty of Being* (published by Coward-McCann) and in that version appeared in *Status*—the same version which is here reprinted.

N. R.

New York, 1968

THE BEATLES

•

I'm taking the time for a number of things
That weren't important yesterday.

—JOHN LENNON

I NEVER GO TO CLASSICAL CONCERTS ANY MORE,
and I don't know anyone who does. It's hard still to care whether
some virtuoso tonight will perform the *Moonlight Sonata* a bit
better or a bit worse than another virtuoso performed it last
night.

I do often attend what used to be called avant-garde recitals,
though seldom with delight, and inevitably I look around and
wonder: What am I doing here? What am I learning? Where
are the poets and painters and even composers who used to
flock to these things? Well, perhaps what I'm doing here is a
duty, keeping an ear on my profession so as to justify the joys
of resentment, to steal an idea or two, or just to show charity
toward some friend on the program. But I learn less and less.
Meanwhile the absent artists are home playing records; they are
reacting again, finally, to something they no longer find at
concerts.

Reacting to what? To the Beatles, of course—the Beatles, whose arrival has proved one of the most healthy events in music since 1950, a fact which no one sensitive can fail to perceive to some degree. By healthy I mean alive and inspired—two adjectives long out of use. By music I include not only the general areas of jazz, but those expressions subsumed in the categories of chamber, opera, symphonic: in short, all music. And by sensitive I understand not the cultivated listening ability of elite Music Lovers so much as instinctive judgment. (There *are* still people who exclaim: "What's a nice musician like you putting us on about the Beatles for?" They are the same who at this late date take theater more seriously than movies and go to symphony concerts because Pop insults their intelligence, unaware that the situation is now precisely reversed.) As to what occurred around 1950, that will be the starting concern of this brief essay, an essay with a primarily musical approach. Most of the literary copy devoted to the Beatles extols the timely daring of the group's lyrics while skirting the essential, the music. Poetry may be the egg from which the nightingale is hatched, though in the last analysis the nightingale must come first.

My "musical approach" will be that of what once was termed the long-hair composer, somewhat disillusioned, nourished at the conservatory yet exposed all his life (as is any American, of necessity) to jazz. It will not pretend to a total appraisal, only to the fact that I and my colleagues have been happily torn from a long antiseptic nap by the energy of rock, principally as embodied in the Beatles. Naturally I've grown curious about this energy. What are its origins? What need does it fill? Why should the Beatles—who seem to be the best of a good thing, who in fact are far superior to all the other groups who pretend to copy them, most of which are nevertheless American and perpetuating what once was an essentially American thing—why should the Beatles have erupted from *Liverpool*? Could it be true, as Nat Hentoff suggests, that they "turned millions of American adolescents onto what had been here hurting all the time . . . but the young here never did want it raw so they absorbed it through the British filter"? Do the Beatles hurt indeed? And are they really so new? Does their attraction, be it pain or pleasure, stem from their words—or even from what's called their *sound*—or quite plainly from their tunes? Those are the questions, more or less in order, that I'd like to examine.

•

Around 1940, after a rather undifferentiated puberty, American music came into its own. Composers burgeoned over the land which, then deprived of foreign fertilizer, began producing an identifiably native fruit. By the war's end we had cultivated a crop worthy of export, for every branch of the musical tree was thriving: symphonies of all shapes were being ground out in dozens; opera concepts were transplanting themselves into midwestern towns; and, for consideration here, vocal soloists were everywhere making themselves heard. On one side were Sinatra, Horne, Holiday, stylists of a high order, gorgeously performing material whose musical value (when not derived from the Twenties of Gershwin or Porter) was nevertheless middling and whose literary content was dim. On the other side were specialized concert singers—Frijsh, Fairbank, and Tangeman— who, though vocally dubious, still created a new brand of sound by persuading certain youngish composers to make singable songs based on texts of quality.

By 1950 the export was well under way. But our effervescence soon flattened when we realized that no one abroad cared much. Jazz, of course, had always been an attraction in the Europe that dismissed American "serious" music as not very serious; Europe, after all, was also reawakening after two numb decades under Hitler's shadow. But that awakening was into the past, namely into the dodecaphonic system which in America had atrophied, and in Germany had been forgotten by the war. This device (no, not a device but a way of thinking, a philosophy) was being revitalized not in the Germany where it had all begun, but in

France, of all places! By 1950 Pierre Boulez had singlehandedly cleared the path and set the tone that music would follow for the next decade throughout the world. And America took the cue, allowing her new-found individuality to dissolve into what ultimately became the bandwagon of International Academicism.

This turn of events surprised no one more than everyone, namely our most personal and famous composers. The lean melodism conscientiously forged by Aaron Copland, which had become the accepted American Style, was now tossed out by the young. The complicated romantic Teuton soup in which music had wallowed for a century was, in the Twenties, reacted against either by the Spartan purification of a Satie or a Thomson (wherefrom Copland's "Americanism") or by the laughing iconoclasm of Dada which—though primarily, like Surrealism, a painters' and poets' medium—was musically exemplified in certain works of *Les Six*. Now in the Fifties complex systems were revived, literally with a vengeance by certain of the middle-aged (Elliott Carter, Milton Babbitt, Arthur Berger, etc.) whom fame had by-passed during the Coplandesque Forties, and by the young in general. If Dada randomness was reanimated by John Cage, this time with a straight face, Copland himself now chose to become re-engaged in serial formality, also with a straight face, as though intimidated by those deadly serious composers half his age.

These "serious" youngsters, in keeping with the times, were understandably more geared to practical concerns of science than to "superfluous" considerations of Self Expression. When they wrote for the human voice (which they did less and less) it was treated not as an interpreter of poetry—nor even necessarily of words—but as a mechanism, often electronically revamped. Verse itself was no longer married *to* the music, or even framed *by* the music, but was illustrated *through* the music. And there was little use left for live singers.

Live singers themselves, at least those of formal training, weren't interested anyway. Modern music was too difficult. Besides it had no audience, and neither any more did the classical song recital so beloved in the already distant years of Teyte and Lehmann. Young singers were lured away from *lieder*, from *la mélodie*, from their own American "art song," until not one specialist remained. They had all been seduced by the big money and hopeful celebrity of grand opera. Even today the few exceptions are European: Schwarzkopf, Souzay, Fischer-Dieskau. Our accurate Bethany Beardslee certainly makes no money, while her excellent west-coast counterpart, Marni Nixon, now does movie dubbing and musical comedy. But most modern song specialists have awful voices and give vanity concerts for invited guests.

Elsewhere was developing the Progressive, or Cool, jazz of Brubeck and Kenton and Mulligan, a rarefied expression that permitted neither song nor dance. The Hit Parade was defunct, Negro stylists out of jobs, and vulgar vocalists of college bands in low esteem. Song was out.

Meanwhile the wall separating so-called classical from so-called jazz was crumbling, as each division sought somehow to join with and rejuvenate the other. Yet the need for "communication" so widely lamented today seemed to be satisfied less through music—any music—than through other outlets, particularly movies. Movies, in becoming accepted as a fine art, turned out to be the one medium which could depict most articulately the inarticulateness of today, even to intellectuals. Whereas the intellectualization of music had ironically alienated the intellectual and has not much interest for anyone else. Stravinsky, for example, may be a household word, but in fact little that he has composed since 1930, and virtually nothing since 1950, is in the concert repertory anywhere. Stravinsky's recent music is heard exclusively when accompanied by the visuals of Balanchine, when performed biannually by Robert Craft (the presence of the master himself at these performances being the drawing card), or when conducted by the composer on Columbia Records with whom he has an exclusive contract.

I and a handful of song-writing friends (Paul Bowles, Daniel

Pinkham, William Flanagan, David Diamond), who began in the Forties, I consider as having come in at the end, as having attempted the irrelevant resuscitation of a creature with sleeping sickness. Most of us have written depressingly few songs lately, and those few emerged less from driving need than from ever-rarer commissions extended by die-hard specialists. Since there's little money, publication, recording, performance, or even concern for songs, our youthful enthusiasm for that most gently urgent of mediums has, alas, pretty much dampened.

But if the once-thriving Art of Song has lain dormant since the war, indications now show it restirring in all corners of the world—which is not the same world that put it to bed. As a result, when Song really becomes wide awake again (the sleep has been nourishing), its composition and interpretation will be of a quite different order and for a quite different public.

Since big-time vocalists like Leontyne Price are, for economic reasons, no longer principally occupied with miniature forms, and since "serious" composers like Stockhausen are, for scientific reasons, no longer principally occupied with human utterances (of which singing is the most primitive and hence the most expressive), and since a master like Stravinsky (who anyway was never famed for his solo vocal works) seems only to be heard when seen, the artful tradition of great song has been transferred from elite domains to the Beatles and their offshoots who represent—as any nonspecialized intellectual will tell you—the finest communicable music of our time.

This music was already sprouting a decade ago through such innocent male sex symbols as Presley in America and Johnny Halliday in France, both of whom were then caricatured by the English in a movie called *Expresso Bongo*, a precursor of *Privilege*, about a none-too-bright rock singer. These young soloists (still functioning and making lots of money) were the parents of more sophisticated, more *committed*, soloists like Dylan and Donovan, who in turn spawned a horde of masculine offspring including twins (Simon and Garfunkel, the most cultured), quintuplets (Country Joe & The Fish, the most exotic), sextuplets (The Association, the most nostalgic), even septuplets (Mothers of Invention, the most madly satirical). With much less frequency were born female descendants such as Janis Ian or Bobbie Gentry (each of whom has produced one, and only one, good song—and who may be forgotten or immortal by the time this is read) and the trio of Supremes. Unlike their "grandparents," all of these groups, plus some twenty other fairly good ones, write most of their own material, thus combining the traditions of 12th-century troubadours, 16th-century madrigalists, and 18th-century musical artisans who were always composer-performers—in short, combining all sung expression (except opera) as it was before the twentieth century.

For this expression one must now employ (as I have been doing here) the straight-forward word Song, as opposed to the misleading *lieder* which applies just to German repertory, or the pretentious "art song" which no longer applies to anything. (The only designation in English that ever really distinguished "serious art song" from what used to be named "pop tune" was "recital song.") Now, since pop tunes as once performed by such as Billie Holiday and the Big Band during an epoch not merely dormant but dead, are heard not only in night club and theater but in recital and concert, and since those tunes are as good as—if not better than—anything "serious" being composed today, the best cover-all term is simply Song. The only subcategories are Good and Bad. Curiously, it is not through the suave innovations of our sophisticated composers that music is regaining health, but from the old-fashioned lung exercise of gangs of kids.

That the best of these gangs should have come from England is unimportant; they could have come from Arkansas. The Beatles' world is just another part of the undifferentiated International Academicism wherein the question is to be Better rather than Different. It seems to me that their attraction has little to do with (as Hentoff implied) "what had here been hurting," but on the contrary with enjoyment.

No sooner does Susan Sontag explain that "the new sensibility takes a rather dim view of pleasure," than we discover her "new" sensibility growing stale. Her allusion was to a breed of suspiciously articulate composers—suspicious because they spend more time in glib justification than in composition—and who denigrate the *liking* of music, the *bodily* liking of it. Indeed, one doesn't "like" Boulez, does one? To like is not their consideration; to comprehend is. But surely fun is the very core of the Beatles' musically contagious expression: the Japanese, the Poles (who ignore the poetic subject matter of suicide and bombs) love them as much as their English-speaking fans; and surely that expression, by the very spontaneous timeliness of its nature, is something Sontag must approve of. The Beatles are antidote to the new (read "old") sensibility, and intellectuals are allowed to admit, without disgrace, that they like this music.

The Beatles are good even though everyone knows they're good, i.e., in spite of those claims of the Under Thirties about their filling a new sociological need like Civil Rights and LSD. Our need for them is neither sociological nor new, but artistic and old, specifically a *renewal*, a renewal of pleasure. All other arts in the past decade have to an extent felt this renewal; but music was not only the last of man's "useless" expressions to develop historically, it is also the last to evolve within any given generation—even when, as today, a generation endures a maximum five years (that brief span wherein "the new sensibility" was caught).

Why are the Beatles superior? It is easy to say that most of their competition (like most everything everywhere) is junk; more important, their betterness is consistent: each of the songs from their last three albums is memorable. The best of these memorable tunes—and the best is a large percentage ("Here,

There and Everywhere," "Good Day Sunshine," "Michelle," "Norwegian Wood" are already classics)—compare with those by composers from great eras of song: Monteverdi, Schumann, Poulenc.

Good melody—even perfect melody—can be both defined and taught, as indeed can the other three "dimensions" of music: rhythm, harmony, counterpoint (although rhythm is the only one that can exist alone). Melody may be described thus: a series of notes of varying pitch and length, which evolve into a recognizable musical shape. In the case of a melody (*tune* means the same thing) which is set to words, the musical line will flow in curves relating to the verse that propels it inevitably toward a "high" point, usually called climax, and thence to the moment of culmination. The *inevitable* element is what makes the melody good—or perfect. But perfection can be sterile, as witness the thousands of 32-bar models turned out yesterday in Tin Pan Alley, or today by, say, Jefferson Airplane. Can we really recall such tunes when divorced from their words?

Superior melody results from the same recipe, with the difference that certain of the ingredients are blessed with the Distortion of Genius. The Beatles' words often go against the music (the crushing poetry that opens "A Day in the Life" intoned to the blandest of tunes), even as Martha Graham's music often contradicts her dance (she gyrates hysterically to utter silence, or stands motionless while all hell breaks loose in the pit). Because the Beatles pervert with naturalness they usually build solid structures, whereas their rivals pervert with affectation, aping the gargoyles but not the cathedral.

The unexpected in itself, of course, is no virtue, though all great works seem to contain it. For instance, to cite as examples only the above four songs: "Here, There, and Everywhere" would seem at mid-hearing to be no more than a charming college show ballad, but once concluded it has grown immediately memorable. Why? Because of the minute harmonic shift on the words "wave of her hand," as surprising, yet as satisfyingly *right* as that in a Monteverdi madrigal like "A un giro sol." The notation of the hyper-exuberant rhythms in "Good Day Sunshine" was as aggravatingly elusive to me as some by Charles Ives, until I realized it was made by *triplets over the bar*; the "surprise" here was that the Beatles had made so simple a process *sound* so complex to a professional ear, and yet (by a third convolution) be instantly imitable by any amateur "with a beat." "Michelle" changes key on the very second measure (which is also the second word): in itself this is "allowed"—Poulenc often did it, and certainly he was the most derivative and correct composer who ever lived; the point is that he *chose* to do it on just the second measure, and that the choice worked. Genius doesn't lie in not being derivative, but in making right choices instead of wrong ones. As for "Norwegian Wood," again it is the arch of the tune—a movement growing increasingly disjunct, an inverted pyramid formed by a zigzag—which proves the song unique and memorable, rather than merely original.

The Beatles' superiority, of course, is finally as elusive as Mozart's to Clementi: both spoke skillfully the same tonal language, but only Mozart spoke it with the added magic of genius. Who will define such magic? The public, in realizing this superiority, is right, though not, as usual, for the wrong reason—as it was, say, ten years ago with *Lolita*. For while *Lolita* was accepted pretty much as just a naughty novel, the Beatles can legitimately be absorbed by all ages on all levels: one is allowed to dance or smoke or even have a funeral (playwright Joe Orton's in London) while listening to this music. The same public when discussing the Beatles does not do so by relating them to others, but by relating them to aspects of themselves, as though they were the self-contained definition of an entire movement, or as though in their so-brief career they had (which is true), like Picasso or Stravinsky, already passed through and dispensed with several "periods." For example, no sooner was the Sergeant Pepper album released than a quiver of argument was set off as to whether it was inferior to their previous album *Revolver*, or to *Rubber Soul*. The Beatles, so to speak, had sired themselves. But was "Eleanor Rigby" their mother or daughter? was "Michelle" their grandmother or granddaughter? and was the She of "She's Leaving Home" perhaps a sister, since she was the most recently born, or a wife?

And what's this one hears about their sound, those psychedelic effects produced from orchestration "breakthroughs" presumably inspired by Paul McCartney's leanings toward Stockhausen and electronics? Well, as first demonstrated in "Tomorrow Never Knows" and "Strawberry Fields," the sound proves less involved with content than color, more with glamor than construction. McCartney's composition has not been affected by these "innovations" which are instrumental tricks glossily surrounding the composition. Nor is any aspect of that composition itself more "progressive" than the Big Bands of yore, or the Cool groups of yesterday. The harmony at its boldest, as with the insistent dissonances of "I Want to Tell You," is basically Impressionist and never more advanced than the Ravel of *Chansons Madécasses*. The rhythm gets extremely fancy, as in "Good Day Sunshine," but nearly always falls within a 4/4 measure simpler than the simplest Bartók of fifty years ago. The melodies, such as "Fixing a Hole" or "Michelle," are exquisitely etched, but evolve from standard modes—those with the lowered thirds and sevenths of the Blues. The counterpoint when strict, as in parts of "She's Leaving Home" is no more complex than "Three Blind Mice," and when free, as in "Got to Get You into My Life," has the freedom of Hindemith—which is really Bach without the problems, meaning without the working out of the solutions presented by the rigors of 18th century part-writing. (The Supremes, not to mention instrumentalists like Ornette Coleman, go much farther out than the Beatles in this domain). As for the overall form, the songs of *Sergeant Pepper* are mostly less complicated than those of previous albums which, themselves, seldom adventured beyond a basic verse/chorus structure. It is not in innovation that Paul McCartney's originality lies, but in superiority. It remains to be seen how, if ever, he deals with more spacious forms. But of that miniature scene, Song, he is a modern master. As such he is the Beatles' most significant member.

The lyrics, or rather the poems, of John Lennon have been psychoanalyzed beyond recognition. They are indeed clever, touching, appropriately timely, and (which is most important) well mated with the tunes. Yet without the tunes, are they really all that much better than the words of, say, Cole Porter or Marc Blitzstein? Certainly Blitzstein's music succeeds in spite of the dated commentary of his words, and Porter's songs remain beautiful with no words at all. We are often told (for instance by Korall in *Saturday Review*) that the Beatles "are shouting about important things," but are these things any more pertinent than "Strange Fruit" yesterday or "Miss Otis Regrets" the day before? was Peggy Lee's crooning "Where or When" less psychedelic than "Lucy in the Sky"? And even if they are, could that be what makes the Beatles good? While the film *Privilege* portrays a rock singer so subversive he requires total control, the fact is, as Gene Lees puts it, that "thus far no rock group, not even the entire rock movement put together, has made a government nervous, as Gilbert and Sullivan did." Even if, in a pinch, poems can be successfully political, no music can be proved to "signify" anything, neither protest, nor love, nor even bubbling fountains, nothing. John Lennon's words do indeed not only expose current problems ("A Day in the Life") but suggest solutions ("Fixing a Hole"); and the music—which is presumably set to the verse, not vice versa—works fine. But that music is stronger; and, like the slow and meterless Gregorian Chant which altered the "meaning" of the rapid and ribald street chanties it stemmed from, Lennon's words do or don't matter according to how they're sung.

With Billie Holiday it was not so much the song as her way with the song; like Piaf she could make mediocrity seem masterful. With the Beatles it's the song itself, not necessarily their way—like Schubert whom even a monster can't destroy. "Michelle," for example, remains as lovely but becomes more clearly projected when performed by a "real" singer like Cathy Berberian. Her diction (and the diction of nearly anyone) is better than theirs, at least to non-cockney ears. Even if the words did not come second, the Beatles oblige you to judge the music first, by virtue of their blurred enunciation.

As for George Harrison's excursions into India, they seem the least persuasive aspect of the more recent Beatle language. Like McCartney with electronics, Harrison seems to have adopted only the frosting; but in pretending to have adopted also the structure, his two big pieces, "Love You To" and "Within You Without You," end up not hypnotic, merely sprawling. Harrison's orientalism is undoubtedly sincere but sounds as fake as the pentatonicism of Country Joe & The Fish. Debussy, like all his cohorts, was profoundly influenced by the Balinese exhibits at the Paris World's Fair of 1900, which inspired his *Pagodes* and *Lindaraja*. These pieces were as persuasive in the same genre as were the concert works many decades later by Henry Cowell or Harry Partch or even Peggy Glanville-Hicks. But whereas these sophisticated musicians without concern for "authenticity" translated Eastern sound effects into Western jargons and then spoke those jargons with controlled formality, Harrison still flounders for faithful meaning where it just won't work: good will and "inspiration" will never provide him with the background—the birthright—which of necessity produced the music he would emulate.

Ringo Starr's projects, when not involved with his comrades, are unknown, though he does seem to be learning to sing with what is quite literally an unutterable charm. Nor have I seen John Lennon's war movie. Thus far, however, when the Beatles are a conjointly creative process (even more than as a performing unit) they are at their most interesting.

Just as today my own composition springs more from pristine

necessity than driving inspiration (I compose what I want to hear because no one else is doing it), so I listen—sifting and waiting—only to what I need. What I need now seems less embodied in newness than in nostalgia: how many thrilling experiences do we get per year anyway, after a certain age? Such nostalgia appears most clearly engendered by the Beatles. There isn't much more to say, since structurally they're not interesting to analyze: they've added nothing new, simply brought back excitement. The excitement originates (other than, of course, from their talent) in their absolutely insolent—hence innocent—unification of music's disparate components—that is, in using the most conservative devices of harmony, counterpoint, rhythm, melody, orchestration, and making them blend with a contagious freshness. (Parenthetically, their latest, "I Am a Walrus," seems a bit worrisome, more contrived, less "inspired" than anything hitherto. Though the texture may be Vaughan Williams with a Bebop superimposition and all very pretty, the final effect becomes parody of self-parody, the artist's realest danger. Though probably even the holy Beatles must be permitted an occasional stillborn child.)

The Beatles have, so to speak, brought *fiction* back to music, supplanting criticism. No, they aren't new, but as tuneful as the Thirties with the same exuberance of futility that Bessie Smith employed. They have removed sterile martyrdom from art, revived the sensual. Their sweetness lies in that they doubtless couldn't care less about these pedantic explications.

If (and here's a big If) music at its most healthy is the creative reaction of, and stimulation for, the body, and at its most decadent is the creative reaction of and stimulation for the intellect—if, indeed, health is a desirable feature of art, and if, as I believe, the Beatles exemplify this feature, then we have reached (strange though it may seem as coincidence with our planet's final years) a new and golden renaissance of song.

Afterthoughts on the Beatles

Will you still need me, will you still feed me,
When I'm sixty-four?

—JOHN LENNON

Dear Sir—

The two major (there are innumerable minor) flaws in Richard Goldstein's criticism of the Beatles—and which render it undependable as well as (what's worse) square, despite his hip style—are condemnation by comparison, and inability to get to the point.

To state that one Beatles record is historically superior to another is both premature and irrelevant; each is self-contained and must now be judged as such. The judgment will not be consideration of side issues like instrumentation or, yes, even words, but consideration of the essential: the tune.

One example will suffice. For Goldstein to disparage "She's Leaving Home" as an imitation of "Eleanor Rigby" is unfair: the songs are independent, incomparable. If one *must* compare them, the *point* is that "Eleanor Rigby," though set to a poem of touchingly original and quasi surrealist winsomeness, is a tune predictable and banal as the average Kentucky carol. "She's Leaving Home," while set to less compelling verse, is a mazurka equal in melancholy and melodic distinction to any of Chopin's. Real musicians, and history too, judge music by musical standards.

Ned Rorem

That letter was addressed to *The Village Voice* and reproduced therein during July 1967. As a result, *The New York Review of Books* commissioned the foregoing article. During its composition I learned a good deal more about the Beatles than I cared to know. I also thought about music in general which hadn't much obsessed me for years. What follows here then is a random series of deletions and postscripts. Because, like most composers, my thoughts go in and out of focus, shift, vanish like slippery prize fish that return as worthless mongrels. But one grows attached even as opinions sicken and metamorphose. It's hard to clean house.

•

When observing careers in the making, a conflict arises in both enthusiasts and detractors: they get so concerned with what *should* be developing that they grow blind to what *is* developing; they aggrandize themselves by showing what *they* would have done, while neatly ignoring what, in fact, was done. If we can already situate in retro-perspective our homegrown performing talents like Maria Callas and Ava Gardner, or creative ones like Tennessee Williams and Jerome Robbins, we are still witnessing the unfolding gifts of, say, Alfred Chester or Andy Warhol, whose works are not sufficiently distant for us to sort the wheat from their chaff. We are cruel to shrink an artistic generation to a five-year span, and to demand always something novel from our artists without allowing them to crib even from themselves. As though any artist ever really "said" more than two or three things in his whole life! He repeats himself continually, perhaps with varied colors and formats, but with the same recurring obsessions.

We've grown intimidated by bright critics, who in turn have been brainwashed by that breed I named "suspiciously articulate composers." Suspicious, because they place understanding before feeling. (Paradoxically, understanding has never before been a prerequisite of art appreciation any more than of love; in fact, once we *understand* our love—once its mystery is clarified—that love ironically evaporates. But then, love is no longer a question in art either.)

The bright critics meanwhile, vengeful of the intimidation, hate to let an artist get too big for his britches.

•

They speak of the artist's responsibility. But he has none, even to himself. Responsibility's a moral question, art isn't. Unlike ethics, art doesn't seek to change so much as confirm: art renders us more so. Should it manage to change us, it would fail as art, nor could it ever succeed so well as philosophic propaganda— the lucid logic of words and deeds. Ritual, being narcotic, changes us; art, being a cleanser, establishes us. The Beatles know that art evolves from ritual, but they do not confuse art with ritual, as do the inferior popsters. Politics rise and fall, but the work of art presumably goes on forever (it may change meaning from age to age, but not shape: the *fact* of it is stationary).

Responsibility? Artists will feel no guilt about not giving the public what it wants, though they may feel guilty about giving the public what it *does* want (e.g. what it expects), about being coerced, entertaining, condescending. Artists, after all, are the makers of manners. The performer may have a responsibility toward the composer, but the composer has none toward the performer beyond the practical one of making his music performable on some terms. Since with the Beatles composer and performer are one (or four, shall we say), that particular rift is bridged. Indeed, if for the bourgeois, Artist now means so much it means nothing, for Youth which dictates the tone of any generation Art and Artist are no longer capitalized: art is where they find it, in museums or mountains, Buxtehude or the Beatles, formed by what they call The Environment rather than by one ego signed in large letters. The Youth Public itself has come to be less judge than participant in what is no longer good and bad Art, just good and bad.

•

Lolita? Coincidentally, are not the Beatles, at first sound, like a choir of male nymphets?, like the long-silent castrati of Handel's day evolving through Tom Sawyer via Balthus?, or like Tchelitchew's leaf-children come to life with androgynous cries echoing all through the tree of Hide & Seek, not asking but forcing us to listen again?

•

Reaction to "intellectualism" came in the fifties through the purple pleasure of nearly all painters retreating from methods of obscurantism by no longer avoiding "communication" as a dirty word (the same painters who now eschew the easel in favor of film-making and choreography), through the poems of Ginsberg and Kenneth Koch, and through the novels of Durrell and Nabokov. Music, as always, lagged behind like an abandoned child, a lost but pompous Fauntleroy nobody cared about any more.

•

No, Europe never took American "serious" music very seriously. France still doesn't, but that makes little difference since France has surrendered to Germany her rôle as musical tastemaker. Of course today the only music taken seriously by anyone serious anywhere is that of the Beatles.

•

Yes, the revitalization of dodecaphonism recommenced not in Germany but in France. One doesn't think of France as latching onto "systems"—schools, perhaps (Impressionism, Surrealism, Dada), but not systems. Though, of course, it is not countries but individuals who make rules in art.

•

The Beatles indicate. The pendulum will not swing back, but it may swing all the way around (if the world lasts), at which time music will quit the artificial confines of concert halls and again become what it was before the Industrial Revolution—an art for what sounds like a contradiction in terms: the aristocratic populace.

•

What is their genre?

In *Music From Inside Out* I distinguished France from America as follows: The French popular song has triple meter with narrational subject matter in A-B-C form. The American popular Song has duple meter with static subject matter in A-B-A form. Americans relate a state of mind, the French a state of body. The difference between America and France is, in the largest sense, the difference between Protestant specialists and Catholic non-specialists.

The Beatles, being English, straddle the ocean by describing little situations, or storylets, which develop, which "happen" (but which are certainly less than Piaf-type sagas), and they do it in both duple and triple meter. (True, *All You Need Is Love* starts out in 7/4, but that comes off as a gimmick no more adventuresome than Tchaikowsky, and anyway it doesn't relate a story.)

The genre is semi-narrational.

•

Their autonomy seems no longer required for their success, or even for their personality. The much publicized branching out is indicative, because clearly good, though as yet uncertain.

Paul McCartney's score to *The Family Way* might have been on a par with Satie's *Entr'acte* or Copland's *Of Mice And Men*; like them it was not a flow of Wagnerian molasses shadowing the action, but a series of functional "set numbers" (three, I think, if a single hearing could judge) as neat as those in a Purcell opera. Might have been—but was not. It seemed clear that although the young composer provided an uncut jewel of highest quality, it remained for some "professional" to polish, shatter, and set that jewel. The music was disseminated throughout the film with a gratuitously psychological "rightness," sometimes omitted where most needed (when the hero upstairs ponders, while downstairs a contrasting bewilderment occurs— a duet-situation Copland dealt with so touchingly in *The Heiress*), sometimes decorative where least needed, as in the tasteless finale. Had the dirty work (i.e.—arrangement, orchestration, and dramatic juxtaposition of the raw material) been left to McCartney, it is tempting to speculate on his ingenuity; for if music can't actually ruin a movie (though in *Doctor Zhivago*, say, or *Baby Jane*, it tries hard) it *can* enhance or radically alter a movie's complexion, or even a movie's intent (as in *The Blood of a Poet*). However clever McCartney's inventions may have turned out—given his technical compositional know-how—the ultimate result would still have proved nothing beyond his instinct for fine points of theater. How much, anyway, should a composer *know?* Some of our greatest show tunes were composed by the likes of Irving Berlin or Noël Coward, proud of their ignorance of even musical shorthand. Such presumption, if such it may be called, now pervades the long-hair world forcing definitions to change at breakneck speed. As to the age-old query about who enjoys music more, the professional or the amateur, that must remain as insoluble as: Who has more fun in love-making, man or woman?—at least until an auditory Teresias shows up. For myself, I no longer hear new music except visually: if it pleases me I inscribe it on a staff in the brain, photograph that notation, take it home and develop the film which can be preserved indefinitely. This manner of musical recall is not, I think, unusual to many composers.

•

How soon will these words be dated? How soon, indeed, will anyone's! Or my diaries, for that matter? or myself? Or this universe?

The fact is, I'm already wearying of the Beatles, resenting the pompous elation their efforts effect in the hearts of my friends. Already wearying, true to my times, as one gets with anything that becomes too In. And need to return toward that hermitage, again to meditate upon, and then compose, something of my own.

BERNAC AND POULENC

•

I have sought neither to ridicule nor to mimic tradition, but to compose naturally as I felt impelled to.

—POULENC

AROUND TWENTY YEARS AGO, BEFORE THE funeral bells of Song began to toll, a very Parisian team, and the ultimate in their art, arrived in America for a first visit. They were composer-pianist Francis Poulenc with his longtime colleague Pierre Bernac, baritone-musician, and they had come to present a group of recitals in Town Hall. I can still remember the photograph used for their advance publicity: the two gentlemen were standing informally and gazing straight into the lens with daguerreotype Gallic grins as broad as Fernandel's. What a contrast to the still standard American pose of an artist absorbed in a score that speaks to him of his serious craft! And what a promise of humor, sensuality, fresh air!

The general public over here didn't then know much of Poulenc's larger work; indeed, not until after his premature death in 1963 did certain of our Big Critics conclude that, well, he wasn't all just perfume and frivolous frills. But if he was already famous through small piano pieces (especially, to his annoyance, the *Mouvements perpetuels*), his reputation had really preceded him across the ocean on wings of song. Poulenc was the undisputed master of the medium. Every qualified vocal teacher taught his *mélodies*, every imaginative American recitalist (there were several) sang them, every voice-minded composer learned them by heart, and every tasteful collector returned from a first postwar trip to France with records this pair had been producing since they joined forces in 1935. No wonder Town Hall was packed to the rafters on this occasion, and on subsequent ones for the next few years, with the international gold of that dusky *belle époque*: Povla Frijsh, Eva Gauthier, Maggie Teyte, the young Tourel, and local ladies like dear Nell Tangeman, Janet Fairbank, Mina Hager, with their hundreds of followers.

As a result of his world tours with Poulenc, Pierre Bernac quickly became *the* authority on French Song and on the poetry to which it was set. If Americans, who usually specialize, are taught to sing (badly) every language but their own, Bernac, like all Europeans (usually general practitioners) mastered his own tongue first and foremost. To this day no student genuinely concerned with either *mélodies* or *chansons* (there aren't many left, *hélas*) can count himself equipped without a trip to the Avenue de la Motte-Piquet to coach with the master.

That master has never been famed for the gorgeousness of his voice—or rather his *voices*, for primarily he is an actor, a multi-masked *diseur*; much of the vocality is actually faked (especially high notes), smoothed over with poignant suavity and with the tastefully vulgar twang of Opéra Comique. Bernac's chief quality was, and is, that he knows what he's singing about, and how to persuade you that his version is definitive. He does this through a flawless, if sometimes coy, diction; he does it, so (literally) to speak, by *reciting* the verse as already re-etched in its lowest terms by Poulenc (or Gounod or Chabrier), not by interpreting, i.e.—adding to, it; and he does it by molding those economically near-literal repetitions in such manner that they are never twice the same. All of which, I suppose, is what makes French music French. (Although, parenthetically, why French music should be deemed by those who don't need it—even by some who do—as non-physical, as antiseptically formal, as sophisticatedly anti-sensual, seems incomprehensible. I, for one, truly swoon, again and again, over the tunes and harmonies of *Daphnis* or *Jeux*, of the *Carmélites* or even *Socrate*.)

Similarly, Francis Poulenc knew what he was composing about. In the tradition of Satie out of Fauré (the first he adored, the second he loathed—perhaps because he saw himself too closely mirrored) he set words to music according to the dramatic dictates of the text, though without Micky-Mousing, and according to the century of the poet. His songs *spoke*, most often with a so-French note-to-note syllabification, as opposed to the more melismatic Italian style. He was probably the most eclectic composer who ever lived, borrowing undisguisedly from a hodge-podge of tried and true languages. Yet in speaking those languages with an accent instantly indentifiable as his, he proved them far from exhausted.

As to his accompaniments, they are sometimes precisely that. More often the piano interweaves itself as a conversational filigree with the voice, Debussy-style, or plays along in unison, Schubert-style. His personal execution of these accompaniments was not in the self-effacing genre of the habitual hired pianist who puts down the "soft pedal" at the concert's start and lets it up at the end. No, he shared, chattered, sometimes dominated. And his chattering shared domination was never so well matched as when he concertized with Pierre Bernac.

In that already faraway quarter-century before 1960 during which Poulenc and Bernac functioned as a professional team, they recorded the composer's complete piano-vocal and chamber-vocal works (some of them many times), as well as the main baritone (or more properly *baryton martin*) repertory of 19th-century Germany and of 19th- and 20th-century France. Two recitals culled from the last category have now been reissued* and are the purpose of this discussion.

The first recital was recorded over the beginning decade of their affiliation and contains a mixed bag from Gounod to Auric. There is no condescension in the artists' approach to a non-Poulenc repertory: it shines with both responsibility and love, and with the venerable elegance that comes from possessing such music in throat, fingers, and heart since childhood. Nevertheless, of nineteen songs by the ten composers represented, it becomes Poulenc's own *Montparnasse*—his realization of Apollinaire's lonely words and Bernac's understanding of that realization—which most strikes home. (The composer once noted in his yet-unpublished *Journal de mes mélodies* that this 3-page song, composed over a period of four years, had cost him great strain. You'd never know it!)

Other representations seem pale to me today, especially the Gounod which tediously promises to hatch from its honeyed cocoon but never does, and the Chausson, both words and music of which grow distant in a way that no longer makes a difference. Chabrier, of course, is the personal joy of all Frenchmen, a joy that (like Pushkin for Russians) never bridged the frontiers. Three famous songs each by Fauré and Duparc are included, and a pair by Roussel sounding a bit too close for comfort like the gorgeous Ravel which follows. As for the Milhaud and Auric contributions, they must have been chosen less out of malice than charity for two partners in crime from the heyday of *les Six*.

The mechanical sound is far from perfect, and Bernac declared last year that this disk's overall point of view didn't always

---

* Bernac and Poulenc: *Mélodies* (Pathé)
  Bernac and Poulenc: *Recital* (Odyssey)

jibe with his current approach. Yet his voice was never to sound fresher, and certainly Poulenc's pianism was exemplary, if occasionally too toned down.

His piansim is occasionally too toned up on the other record, but like most composers I rather approve. This second recital is more successful; also more inclusive, being two disks (containing goodly slices of Debussy and Ravel, the father and mother of modern France, and three large cycles by Poulenc himself); the sound is closer to what we've grown accustomed to; and the performance represents the peak of the team's expressive powers in 1950 during the American successes.

The *Histoires naturelles* were performed in 1907 by their composer Maurice Ravel, with soprano Jane Bathori who, at least until recently, was still living in Paris. No doubt Madame Bathori passed on some pointers from the horse's mouth to Monsieur Bernac: it is hard now to imagine this cycle as having a legitimate reading by anyone but him: from his impersonation of the pompous peacock to the giddy Guinea hen he literally inhabits the bird kingdom, from which he emerges with a startling new voice as a Jewish cantor in the same composer's Hebrew Songs.

Chabrier's *L'Île heureuse*, which adorned the other disk, is repeated here as an appetizer to five Debussy masterpieces and three goodies by Satie. *Calligrammes*, a suite of seven Apollinaire poems as musicalized by Francis Poulenc, was premiered at those famous New York concerts. It is full of contrast and ingenuity, but glibber and less immediately opulent or theatrical than his two earlier cycles, *Banalités* and *Chansons Villageoises*. In those one's spine turns to glass at such music as "Sanglots" or "Le Mendiant," while songs like "C'est le joli printemps" or "Tu vois le feu du soir" will, thank God, still make us cry.

But our tears are the purging ones of release which ultimately melt into smiles as wide as those of these Frenchmen twenty years ago. Their smiles in retrospect have turned to a laugh, partly the bold laugh of two artists who said they'd been no less influenced by Chevalier than by Mary Garden, and partly the last laugh that symbolized both the end of one communicable epoch and the start of another wherein pleasure, as the word is generally understood, becomes a vanishing criterion.

Afterthoughts on Francis

mais bien je veux qu'un arbre
m'ombrage en lieu d'un marbre
—RONSARD (musicalized by Poulenc in 1924)

We were visiting him, Henri Hell and I, for our sumptuous semi-annual *goûter*, 5 rue de Médicis, on an already darkening autumn afternoon in 1953. The usual meeting with Francis Poulenc was like uncorking a champagne bottle, but that day he had little sparkle and no appetite for the lusty spread of homemade pear tarts and camomile tea. Rubbing the large forehead above his closed eyes, he muttered with a grin of nasal irony: *"Le groupe des Six viéllit!"* (Read: which one of us will be the first to go?) A few months later Honegger died. But nearly a decade passed before the disappearance of the second of The Six—Francis himself.

Immediately I composed a sort of verbal souvenir-portrait. Now that, too, is years ago when aftermaths were not as yet in view.

This composer—whose music, like his life, shifted between

the sophisticatedly bawdy, the vetivered nostalgic, and the genuinely moral and religious and sad (though never "depressed")—left, in the wake of his dying, a sort of chaos personally, and the grandest correction artistically. (The day of his unexpected collapse, letters had all been answered, contracts signed, everything was in order.)

On the one hand—according to the coincidence of hearsay—friends and family and (ironically) offspring suffered death, incarceration, and inheritance complications. On the other, while it is contrary to the "style" of newly deceased composers to be granted sudden fame (as opposed to painters whose market value, by definition, rises when they die), Poulenc nevertheless received an instantly belated quickening of appreciation. Indeed, ask the average Square, or Opera Queen, or Rock Lover, whom —outside his own specialty—he most digs from the present century, and the only name he's likely to come up with (besides Gershwin) is that of Francis Poulenc.

Why? For the same reason that everyone from every class likes the Beatles. Such music makes us feel good, makes us cry, and we're no longer ashamed of these responses.

•

Like the Beatles, or like the novels of, say, James Purdy, which give the lie to the until-recently chic suggestion that criticism has supplanted fiction, the resuscitation of Poulenc de-intellectualizes the art of music in favor of kinetic response. Thank God he's good!

•

Another likeness to the Beatles, one which embarrasses: The Cute Ending. Any number of Poulenc's pet works, especially shorter piano pieces (for instance, the first two *Mouvements perpetuels*), de-dignify themselves with a silly tail. Like "Strawberry Fields" or "All You Need Is Love." With these Beatles songs one blushes at the nuanced interpretations found in Culture Mags. Transpose those interpretations to Poulenc and blush again, not so much at the critic as at the artist-as-apologist—as though he were saying: Don't take my lack of seriousness too seriously. (Gide had it both ways: "Don't be too quick to understand me.")

•

In the Beatles essay I quoted Susan Sontag about how The New Sensibility takes a dim view of pleasure (page 302 of *Against Interpretation*), with her confirming example: "The great contemporary French composer, Pierre Boulez, entitled an important essay of his twenty years ago, 'Against Hedonism in Music.'" Such words patronize at least one reader who feels that Sontag herself reached those conclusions mechanically—only yesterday perhaps—by hearsay: she explains that Boulez is *the great contemporary*, must tell us that his essay is *important*, qualifications which would be superfluous for one on surer ground. Her up-to-dateness renders a dissenter limp; yet is the music she "defends" necessarily necessary because it springs from current scientific "needs"? From what's in the air? Art pays homage to Science, and Science couldn't care less. Can one be simultaneously against interpretation and against hedonism? Then Sontag inadvertently reveals that Boulez' article is already twenty years old. (Boulez meanwhile has become a major conductor of "classics" while his own composition seems at a standstill.) True, pleasure still *is* rather underplayed in the "new" sensibility, but that sensibility is already old.

Oh, how the generations shrink! One brief one contains the wise Susan, another contains me, and a still earlier one contained Francis Poulenc who wrote for the sheer joy of Self Expression (an obscene term in the fifties), a joy which has returned—if only for a few calm moments before the final storm.

•

The dark afternon in 1953, however, was far removed from the joy scene. Musical centuries have, since time began, switched themselves neatly from contrapuntal to harmonic and back again (otherwise stated: holy to un-sacred, brainy to sexy, horizontal to vertical, inhibited to extrovert). Poulenc and the Beatles flow purely from harmony to heavenly harmony; and though the Beatles may profit fully, Poulenc can only smile from heaven. Because 1953 was the climax of a contrapuntal era, an era which continued through the year of his death.

•

The pupil swipes from—and surpasses—his master.

Like an inverted cuckoo, Francis Poulenc welcomed into his nest the eggs of many another songbird from past and present. Once hatched, the offspring took on the colors of their mother Francis, without (mysteriously) altering the least harmony of their various fathers—Couperin, Chopin, Moussorgsky, Fauré, Debussy, Stravinsky, Satie, Ravel.

Ravel's *Une barque sur l'océan* is a lesser work by a great composer. Poulenc's *Figure humaine* is a major work by a lesser composer—or one who used to be termed "lesser." Yet one section from this major work, titled *Toi ma patiente*, is a note-for-note steal from *Une barque*; Poulenc doesn't even bother to change Ravel's key. Nevertheless his choral working-out is superior to Ravel's piano piece, precisely because it *is* a working-out.

•

In that game of If-You-Were-on-a-Desert-Island-with-Only-Five-Records, two of mine would surely be Ravel's *L'Enfant et les sortilèges* and Poulenc's *Stabat Mater*, because they comprise every aspect of the sonorous variables (sung words both solo & choral, and orchestra), and they do it *à la française*, which is my need. I might include *Figure humaine*; not, however, *La Voix humaine*, for, despite its beauty, it always relates the same story, whereas *Figure humaine* changes meaning with each hearing.

•

The day he won the Pulitzer for *Vanessa* Sam Barber came, along with me, to dine at Lee Hoiby's. "Have you heard," I asked, "that Poulenc's writing a monologue for Callas on *La Voix humaine*?"

"Francis is opportunistic."

"Still, it's a swell idea."

"Because Maria's an opportunist—can't stand other singers on stage."

"But still, it's a swell idea. Admit it."

"You think so because you're an opportunist."

"Yes, but still—wouldn't you have wanted her for *Vanessa*?"

"All right. Puncture me where it hurts the most!"

•

But la Callas did not create the role.

Jacques Bourgeois had already played me both recordings of *La Voix humaine*: Berthe Bovy's desperate "silent" version breathed onto wax back in the thirties, and Poulenc's musicalization as realized by Denise Duval who rivaled Callas as our greatest post-war singing actress.

On Friday, September 15, 1961, Jacques took me to see (in Paris one goes to see opera, not hear it) Duval's performance in the half-empty hall *au Comique*. For forty minutes our attention could not quit this small woman, even as a few months ago we were riveted to Dietrich, Dietrich who scarcely moved but who, pernicious cobra, charmed us, mortal sparrows—the only difference being that Duval was a *vulnerable* cobra, striking our hearts while her own heart broke, so simply. So very simply too she moved us during her five-minute walk-on in Dallapiccola's

Vol de Nuit co-billed that night with *La Voix humaine.* (*La Voix humaine!* And during the war years—years which the French call merely *l'occupation*—it was, on Eluard's verse, the massive a-cappella *Figure humaine*, dedicated appropriately, humanly, humanely, to André Dubois who effected the Jewish exodus. Francis, and all that was human equals: Francis, and all that was selfish!) Who wept directly behind us? The *maître* himself. Now at intermission he speaks:

"*Mon petit Ned, est-ce vraiment la première fois que tu l'aies entendue, ma Voix?*" [For he tutoyéd me always, though I in return never knew how to address the idol of my childhood—one so seldom talks with statues] . . . "Tonight's the fiftieth performance. The fiftieth! At every one she interjects something new. You saw how she tore open that pack of Gitanes, took out the cigarette, lit it, inhaled, all the time singing into the receiver crooked under her chin! Never has she smoked before, la Duval, nor should she. Nor should *you*, dear Ned: nor should you drink; anything, *anything* that comes before your work is wrong. You look terrible tonight, eyes wretched as the black hole of Calcutta." [His own orbs, staring into my features, were scarcely more lovely, surrounded in all their abstinent glory of liver spots and moles.] . . . "You need air and sun and a new view of France. Come tomorrow and spend the weekend in Noizay with us, and we'll have two days of promenades and chocolate soufflés."

Next morning at the Gare d'Austerlitz: "No, let's go second class, the people are more fun to watch, thick smells, *les beaux gosses*" [like Colette he used Twenties' expressions], "heavenly banana peels and dungarees—*des salopettes savoureuses. En deuxième* then to Tours, where Raymond will pick us up. . . . What am I composing?" [This, loudly to the whole carload.] "A pointilliste choral piece, pling, pung, just like Boulez but all on white keys! Ah, Boulez—if only I were thirty years younger! Yet I must continue on the road mapped out for me."

The weekend was quiet, quite bourgeois (I've described it elsewhere) except for the formal beauty of Poulenc's miniature chateau, and the absolute richness of the Touraine landscape. During a decade in France I'd known only Paris and Provence, a smattering of Bordeaux, and none of the castle country with those valuable over-all views of a passing traveler. But now la Touraine! the expensive caves of green wine, a thousand clusters of large yellow grapes plucked hot from the vine and smeared juicily through the lips, the endless emerald landscape at the end of summer, such formal gravel paths absent of poverty, wealthy with conversation, and a sunset of accordions evoking those *Soirées de Nazelles* of my host's faraway childhood.

We played our music for each other, he singing like a pregnant bugle his new "La dame de Monte Carlo," I phonographing Phyllis Curtin at song and Lenny Bernstein at my Third Symphony. The constantly reiterated advice of Francis: "Stick with the orchestra, it's your true medium. La Curtin sings French *comme une française*" [he referred to my gymnastic "Jack l'Eventreur"], "but you don't write songs *comme un français*—and that's the only way. No, song is not your real nature, instruments are. *Reste donc chez l'orchestre.*" Self-protectively I accept his motives as *his* self-protection.

●

Who will forget that voice, spoken or sung? the harmless venom, the malignant charity? His indiscriminate choice of friends, yet so discriminately faithful to a type: *la royauté des sergents de ville!*

A few days later, as bread-and-butter gift, I left a rare and fragrant package of Hindu josh sticks (purchased the previous month near Tangier's Xoco Chico) with the concièrge of Poulenc's Paris apartment. On returning to New York the following week I found a letter from Francis thanking me for the incense, which he hoped would light the way toward one of *les beaux flics* which roamed his neighborhood. The smoke, he said, weaved through his yellow plush arm chairs, across the squeaking piano strings, and on out through the casements into the refracting sunlight of the Luxembourg gardens, from whence it might float on the mist of his own song over the Atlantic to America where we would someday meet again. But we never did.

RICHARD STRAUSS

•

*I would like to admit all Strauss operas to whichever
purgatory punishes triumphant banality.*

—STRAVINSKY

AN ARTIST, WE ARE TOLD, IS A KNOT OF SEEMING
contradictions which no philosopher from Socrates to Susanne
Langer has ever been able to unravel. And we are told that, like
everyone, artists struggle between their disordered parts—sacred
and profane, black and white, or whatever—and that their resolution of the struggle becomes a formal offering to the world.
This offering might on one occasion be a Requiem Mass, on
another an erotic ballet, expressions of split personality. (Or was
the artist merely fulfilling the terms of a commission?) Yet who
can prove, especially in wordless music, that there is any "expression" at all? Is art the mirror of its maker, or his magnetized
shadow? Does it lead or follow him? Is it the chicken or the egg?

Must an artist's domestic life resemble, say, that of Debussy,
whose cool sensuality drove women to near suicide while simultaneously defining the texture of his undeniably great music?
Then what of D'Annunzio whose home life was similar but

whose work was inferior? Or Byron? Or Bach, who despite twenty-two children was, as the saying goes, quite normal? (But that was in another time and country, and besides. . .) No, even Freud's conjectures on Leonardo or Dostoevsky are probably irrelevant, if only because in writing of artists he was writing art.

Novelists, along with philosophers and psychoanalysts, are tempted by these questions, especially as they relate to composers who, more than any other so-called creators, appear mysterious to laymen (does that afflatus issue from God or Satan? can a musician really *hear* all those notes in his head?). Yet not even in those fictional essays of dear Romain Rolland or wise Thomas Mann does one find satisfactory clarifications of causal inter-relationships between the social being and his silent greatness. Inspiration, which outsiders always want to hear about, is really beside the point since we are all inspired but we are not all great. It has been said that an artist is like everyone else but no one is like him (like everyone, only more so!). Wherein lies the difference?

Certainly artists themselves have no answers, nor do biographers, although the latter, after the fact, assemble answers that are presumably relevant to something—assuming that any question worth asking has only one reply. No sooner is genius defined than it is contradicted.

A case in point is Richard Strauss, whose only paradox was in his not being a paradox. Not at least in his private life, of which no known element possibly could satisfy a Hollywood concept of artist. He had few struggles, creative or financial, was neither lover nor wit, neither deviate nor jester, touching nor hateful. If for nearly half a century he was the world's most successful composer, he was not even a monster. Nor certainly was he in any sense a hero. Specifically Strauss's life as non-hero becomes the subject of George Marek's recent interesting biography.*

* George R. Marek, *Richard Strauss* (New York: Simon & Schuster, 1967).

Interesting biography of a dull man? How has Marek turned that trick in a book that is more on the person than his music? I suppose by having a sufficiently contagious admiration for the music to want to show the man's very ordinariness as extraordinary. Mr. Marek succeeds. He succeeds not so much by painting a portrait of his subject as a landscape from which that subject emerges: upper middle-class Germany in the latter 1800's. During that period Strauss, although musically famous and fortunate, represented "modern" radicalism; none of his new works was then received without a success *de scandale* as well as *d'estime*. Today with the knowledge of hindsight we recognize his bombast to have been not of innovation but of agony—he wasn't a forerunner but a culminator. One proof might be that no younger composer of value can be pinpointed as having come out of Strauss as Strauss himself came out of Wagner. Doubtless Debussy, if one need name names, opened our twentieth century while Strauss (two years the Frenchman's junior) closed the nineteenth. Indeed, should we continue to treasure him, author Marek feels it will be due to his rôle as the last of the romantics. Being the last of anything seems naturally nostalgic, but it is rather boring.

•

The Bavaria into which Richard Strauss was born is described as a prosperous mixture of nectar and beer, the nectar being exclusively German music which was judged as much for its moral as its artistic worth, and the beer being a certain weighted negligence such as Bülow's magnificent conducting of the Eroica *without a rehearsal*. Some of the nectar was poured by Wagner's gods who reigned over the cultural scene; and some of the beer, at least in Strauss's case, by his own mother whose maiden name of Pschorr was that of Munich's most popular brand. Strauss's father Franz, a great horn player under Wagner (whom he loathed) and a sweetly pleading man, was his son's first mentor, which he remained until death in 1905. He supervised Richard's rapid rise with pride, apprehension, and floods of advice mostly unheeded.

Richard quite early shook off his father's anti-Wagnerianism, adopting the Sage of Bayreuth, along with Mozart, as his most permanent spiritual influence until "Wagner lifted him from Wagner." He shook off less quickly a puerile adherence to his parent's anti-Semitism, a sentiment further quickened through alliance with the famous conductor Bülow. Bülow was not only the most singular sponsor of Strauss' young career but such a powerful figure of the 19th century that he is granted a whole chapter. And the book springs to life. For Bülow's life was one of glittering aphorism and neurotic dedication, of abject devotion (to Wagner—to whom he relinquished his wife), and deadly rivalry. He was a strong champion of progressive causes. To him Strauss owed his first regular employment, that of conductor, a profession which nourished him throughout his life as extensively as his two other vocations of composer and (he hoped) of "gentleman genius."

Another conductor (and anti-Semite), Alexander Ritter, was soon to join Bülow in advancing our non-hero. It was Ritter's belief in "music as expression"—i.e., containing extramusical ingredients—which doubtless turned Strauss to the Tone Poem. That form, if form it may be called, he all but fathered, despite such previous non-verbal storytellers as Berlioz, who at heart was German. It is precisely this avowed or implied need to narrate which lends certain music that plodding quality definable as German, no matter who writes it. By same token Mendelssohn was French in heart, descending from a line of tonal landscapists beginning with Couperin, climaxing in Debussy, and decaying with Respighi and Delius, both of whom must also be considered French.

In 1887 Strauss made the acquaintance of the gentle Gustav Mahler and of the termagant Pauline de Ahna. The former was to remain his faithful colleague although "their natures were antipodal. . . . Mahler was always telephoning to God, while Strauss had his eyes fixed on the world." Pauline was to remain his faithful wife although her viraginous presence forever proved the bane of all but her willingly henpecked husband's existence. She was his only love. To his biographer's admitted disappointment, Strauss was not personally erotic—he let it all out through the music. His abstinence was not maladive however, or "poetic" like, say, Chopin's; perhaps more than any other major composer Strauss lived in the world, his main non-musical preoccupations being self-aggrandizement and money and a card game called Skat. His "image" was far more that of a performer than of a creator, although unlike performers his real-life sensual demands were small.

But his sexual, morbid and heroic compensations through art were elephantine. By 1905 he had produced programmatic works on two Spanish legends, those of the lady-killer Don Juan and the *gaffeur* Don Quixote, another on death, and still another on a hero's life—presumably and ironically his own. He had also composed his third opera which when reduced to lowest terms becomes a pile of scraps, but which as a whole adds up to a compelling horror about the most unbalanced presence of all time: Salomé. It is a masterpiece of civilized barbarity in which Strauss celebrates from afar the first in a series of very perverse ladies.

He had also by now met the first (and best) of his operatic collaborators, the Austrian Hugo von Hofmannsthal. During the next decade the two would invent at least three nearly first-rate dramas, of which certainly *Der Rosenkavalier* must go down in history (despite Stravinsky's delicious remark about it: "How well they go together, bad taste and vigor.")

In his portrait of Hofmannsthal Marek's prose again gains animation. The librettist—like many another subsidiary character—was simply more intriguing and complex than the leading man. Indeed it is the discussion of minor heroes surrounding Strauss, or politico-sociological depictions of the epochs spanned by his life, which make the book readable. The composer was always in contact with people of quality, albeit of Teutonic vintage; artistically he seemed less stubborn than simply incapable of comprehending other than the German mentality, as his correspondence with Rolland would indicate, or his naïve taste in contemporary music. (Taste, of course, like intelligence, is no prerequisite to creativity.)

With the first war came a hiatus of nearly a quarter-century during which—at least as Marek sees it—the composer's ideas ebbed, faltered, and after the death of Hofmannsthal, imitated themselves with other scenarists. He passed through phases more or less dry or fructuous, but never retrieved his early *élan*. His resurgence into genuine originality came only as a kind of swan song after eighty. Assuming that the musical products are enough celebrated to need little elaboration, what then was the master's life during these periods?

Well, he went to America and was a great success. He collaborated with such world figures as Reinhardt, Zweig, Beecham, even Somerset Maugham (who translated *Ariadne*), all most successfully. He discovered Jeritza and Lehmann, who were big successes. In fact, most of what he touched turned to success. He became a classic in his own time, lived a most comfortable life (though he did not seem capable of intimate friendships), and was never never idle. He did good things, such as helping to found the powerful GEMA—which corresponds to our ASCAP —and becoming the active head for many years of the Vienna Opera. He did bad things, such as being—if not downright pro-Nazi—at least indifferent to the horrors. (He was heard to announce: "The Nazis were criminals. Imagine, they closed the theaters and my operas could not be given!" Though in fairness he did once write to Zweig, and during dangerous times, on the subject of Jews: "For me there are only two categories of human beings, those who have talent and those who have not.") He appeared to be quite avid for literary culture despite his manifest vulgarity. His parsimonious conceit was finally no more accentuated than many a lesser artist's. His rather dreary sanity nevertheless produced some thrillingly mad music, for as Marek points out, Strauss was bold. It is Marek's theme however that Strauss as a young composer promised greater genius than was ultimately forthcoming, the reason being that even as the man could not grasp the rhythms of changing eras, so the artist within the man could not survive them.

And even as that man's life palls, so in the end does his music. In my childhood I used to ask how such an untheatrical human could have penned such theatrical scores. Today I ask: Is that music so theatrical? Is all the huffing and puffing, endless explication, overthick orchestration, really so engrossing? Could it be just a heavy reflection of a heavy soul rather than a fanciful contradiction of that soul?

George Marek, although more indulgent than I, does not, with all his just appraisal, unreservedly admire one single work of Strauss. And yet he did write the book. That he wrote it, I repeat, must be because he loved something in the music. What he has given in honor of that love is a fairly valuable sociological study, though he has come no closer than anyone else in demonstrating what makes a composer a composer.

Mostly on French and Germans

*The German is sober, sentimental, and awkward—
all that goes against art. The German is bourgeois;
art is aristocratic.*

—BUSONI

The Strauss review appears in Sunday's *Times*. Early the same morning the phone awakens me, a thick Bavarian accent explodes: "I want you to know that the music of Strauss will still be played long after you and Mr. Marek have turned to dust and ashes."

Many letters came this way as well, all from Germans, hostile or hurt. But I am not anti-German, just un-German.

Is my French orientation due to Quaker background, to a need for silver and perfume of Roman Churches? Certainly from infancy I was drawn toward all things French—*Pelléas, Une saison en Enfer, Le Déjeuner sur l'herbe*—and I celebrated pre-puberty black masses in the privacy of my bed. Yet certainly too, by thirteen, I took to the works of Mann or Wasserman as easily as to those of Flaubert and Gide. Still, it was black hair and the Mediterranean that drew me, not the blond Rhine; a need for sensual economy, not carnal extravagance. So when people ask, "Did all those years in France influence you and your music?" I must answer: I went to France because I was already French, not the other way around. It is not the going home (though we may never have been "home" before) that makes homebodies of us; we are homebodies, so we go home.

•

People are all dogs or cats: as a sex, men are dogs, women cats. Certain men are catlike, of course; but as a whole they're dogs ranging from Chihuahua to Great Dane.

Like nationalities, or races. Negroes are dogs and Orientals are cats, though Orientals in turn are cats and dogs: Chinese are dogs, Japanese are cats. Latins are cats and Anglo-Saxons are dogs. Germans are dogs, the French are cats.

Just as everything's French or German: Negroes are German, Chinese, French; though Chinese are German when Japanese are French. All women are French, all men German. (Can't individual ladies be German?)

Cats are definitely French, though dogs are certainly German, even ladylike Japanese dogs.

Are there no alternatives?

Occasional people are birds or snakes, but all other animals (like horses or gazelles) are sub-categories of German and French, though some Germans are frenchified and vice versa. Of course, painters are doggy and composers catty; oak trees are canine, ferns are feline; feet are Teuton, hands Gallic. Red is a dog and blue is French.

Yes, composers are French—but mostly they're men. The one (and only one) generality for artists is that mostly they're men. Then women say: We've never been given a chance. Were the Jews, the poor, or Abe Lincoln, given a chance? Chances are taken, not given. It's wrong to call women Preying Mantises. The most feminine of the masculine are still more masculine than the most masculine of the feminine; the virilest lady is less male than the gentlest gentleman. Female impersonators feel only a need to prove their womanhood, not manhood, and can change your tire more accurately than the toughest girl.

Richard Strauss was German (let's say that again!), and Germans, alas, are men (aren't they?) for better or worse. Like Gide who, when questioned as to who was France's greatest poet, answered: "Victor Hugo, *hélas!*"

•

What makes the French French? It's hard to put a finger on what makes them French; but I know what makes them not American, and I know that they're quite as innocent about us as we about them, literarily and sociologically. From us they await other Hemingways; though we long ago outgrew (didn't we?) the phony-virility style in favor of words as poetry. Yet when I explain to even the most witty and cultivated Parisian that I was raised in Chicago, he points a finger and says: *"Tu es gangstaire, boum boum!"*

We hear from them that America's the Rome of Europe's Athens. Paul Goodman: "Just this we must, and can, prevent. They really do not know our best [he cites himself]; they know what is notorious and 'successful,' which is of course what their intellectuals seek out and interview. . . Nevertheless, they are probably right about Rome and Athens, and we 'best' are really the new Christians in the mélange."

Robert Phelps tells us that our view of the French (fancy cooking, Folies Bergères, castles-on-the-Loire) is not how they see themselves. "Frenchmen," he notes, "are undeluded, self-sufficing, able to live on very little, unsentimentally efficient about gustatory and sexual satisfaction, firm about property values, keen at survival, and taking profound pride in this."

As for what makes French music French, doubtless it's precisely this essence of thrift—as opposed to German music—

94177

which originates, as I've explained elsewhere (in "Song and Singer"), from speech, which comes from song, which comes from speech, from which comes etc. Basic French thematicism is often either on or within a tetrachord as opposed, say, to those pentatonic formations of the Scotch and Chinese, or highly disjunct Teuton vocal lines.

•

Taste, have they? Well, I may have a sense, though no concern, for interiors, for visual balance, color mixtures, style. But taste I do not have—much less good taste—even in music, as Ravel had and Strauss had not. Nor am I sure that taste is required for genius: it's too controlled. Surely taste is no consideration today, even for specialized audiences whose very eschewing of the attribute has come to be chic.

•

French is the sole romance language without tonic accent—without a heavy fall on one syllable of a two-or-more-syllable word. So in musical settings of French (forgetting standard observances like treating a final mute "e" as a syllable), prosodically anything goes. Thus the natural rise and fall of the spoken tongue is more to be considered. In English, contrariwise, the tonic accent of a multi-syllabic word is stronger than in any other language, so strong indeed that all unaccented syllables are thrown away. Consider the words *telephone* or *only* in which the *-lephone* or the *-ly* are virtually dispensable, as opposed, say, to the Italian (another strongly tonic-accented tongue) *telephono* or *solo* in which the non-accented syllables are nonetheless granted their fair due. The few English exceptions that occur to me, in which both syllables of a two-syllable word are given equal stress, are in the numbers *thirteen* through *nineteen*—doubtless so that the ear may distinguish them from *thirty* and *ninety* wherein the suffix is, of course, nearly inaudible.

•

Linguistics have always intrigued me as much as God, both having been unavailable before reaching France in 1949. If my inclinations had been volatile, my Quaker worship had been mute. The first proper contact with a Parisian man of letters was in Julien Green, bilingual by birth, Catholic by conversion. To whom a more natural enquiry: "When you speak with God, do you speak in French or in English?" He only answered with his eyes, in silence.

ABOUT PETER YATES' BOOK ON TWENTIETH-CENTURY MUSIC

•

> These dishes should add variety to American and British menus. In France they are no longer novelties or creations, nor have they the distinction of being distinctive, which, as defined by a cousin of Gertrude Stein, is something that is done six weeks before all the world is doing it. On the contrary, they are most of them a slow evolution in a new direction, which is the way great art is created—that is, everything about is ready for it, and one person having the vision does it, discarding what he finds unnecessary in the past. Even a way of cooking an egg can be arrived at in this way. Then that way becomes a classical way. It is a pleasure for us, perhaps for the egg. . . It is, of course, understood that there are always those who rush in and irreverently add a dash or a pinch from a bottle, a tin or a package and feel that some needed flavour has been found. This, a matter too literally of taste, is not arguable. It is a pleasure to retire before such a fact.
>
> —The Alice B. Toklas Cook Book

THE BEST MINDS THESE DAYS SEEM MORE geared to commentary than to creation. Certainly our brightest western prose lately has not been fiction but criticism. Painting usually turns out to be less amusing (not to say competent) than the advertising announcing it. As for musical composition, its defense has come to sound more intriguing than itself, even though composer and defender are usually the same.

Peter Yates, so far as I know, is not a composer. He is, how-ever, a Music Lover, which few composers are any more. A Canadian by origin, author of *An Amateur At The Keyboard* and for years a contributor to *Arts and Architecture*, he has long lived in Los Angeles where he founded the now famous "Eve-nings on the Roof." His close acquaintance with the likes of Schoenberg and Stravinsky no less than with others less glamor-ous (mostly west-coasters, it would naturally seem) accounts for his special knowledge of what composers are made of. And it accounts for the dedicated, painstaking and more-or-less objective enthusiasm of his extraordinarily wise book. I can't imagine a composer as having written it—as having had the *time*, the time to care in just this way. And Yates cares.

With care, then, he explains how today's music got that way and how we can learn to take it. He does this by discussing the evolution of all of music's components both as themselves and as exemplified through the works of some dozen key figures of the past century. The discussion is no easy-going appreciation course; the author's intent is not to delight but to instruct, and no such instruction on the current market is more concise. (Thomson's recent portrait is as much of the artist's particular economy as of the general "scene," while Mellers portrayed the scene itself—but only in America.)

Yates is not one of those brainwashed reviewers who, dazed by their own brilliance and the ever-more-quickly changing world, are inclined to confuse the fascination of a work's analysis with the work itself, then to interpret the complexities of that analysis as the work's virtue, and hence to produce false evaluations. "Musical analysts look for what they know, not for what they do not know." Yates knows that the current state of music is not a suddenly random and perverse perpetration of fast thinkers, but the result of a loving and logical growth of selective doers, a growth which (he feels) occurred as an auditory, not a harmonic phenomenon, and has led from the end of the Harmonic Era to the new Era of Sound which will have as its center the computer.

Making it clear at the outset that music and sound can no longer be counter-distinguished, the author proceeds—with his master Schoenberg acting as a sort of invisible Vergil—through the public hells of misunderstanding, touching gently or ponderously most aspects of the subject at hand, through past and present, until he has cleared for us the complex clouds around the hopefully simple paradise of the future. Early we are introduced to the master himself, newly and keenly, "as natural a melodist as Schubert. . . If one were to choose a single work to represent the pre-eminent achievement of twentieth century music until the present day, that work would be [Schoenberg's] *Moses and Aron*." Only Stravinsky is treated so unqualifiedly, in as acute an appraisal as any existing.

We are also reintroduced to Satie whom, of course, it is no longer correct to dismiss as trivial; but he too is shown freshly— as a master of parody, "an aspect of art [wherein] convention and the use of it play at cross-purposes." It was not genius, finally, but energy that Satie lacked. He "created a small art that is completely joyous, not innocent but guiltless, without soil." Without soil, perhaps, but presented utterly as a product of France. Ravel, too, and Debussy are thus presented (yet not as twins, for a change; as polarities). For the psychology of a nation, and resultantly of all forms of that nation's output, is another concern of Yates who quotes Vaughan Williams: "If you subscribe to that . . . foolish description of music as a universal language, you will . . . have achieved nothing better than a standardized . . . cosmopolitanism . . . whose mannerisms you have been aping."

"The student, if he is to master what is taught him, must at the same time challenge it." There is not one hackneyed challenge among Yates' major theses. He speaks at length of the "fourth dimension of sound" (ritualistic audience participation); of Just Intonation (his special obsession); of The Integrity of Compromise ("a great artist, in the long view, creates his audience"; "an artist is not a renegade but a workman"); of The Emancipation of the Dissonance; the beauty of transcriptions as an ancient musical skill ("music is constantly being made new; the notated score is only a guide," although there can be "a regard for the visual score itself as an esthetic object.") "One purpose of hearing music is to enlarge our capacity for listening," yet we are warned that "what gives pleasure is our own tentative recomposing of a type of artistic workmanship with which we have learned to agree!"

The author laments the "dictatorship of popularity" in Russia and America, where "reputation does the work of contemplation," and concludes that this attitude will not soon change. He nevertheless suggests that the past quarter century has been the most fascinating in all musical history, and this period contains the unalterable fact of what John Cage calls "the emancipation of music from its notes."

"Is there esthetic work in a destructive force?" we are asked. "The art of tragedy affirms it." The new language is a "fight against routine." What these days we wearily term " 'lack of communication' has been in reality a slow but steady increase in communication between the serious composer, his travelling representative the conscientious performer, and the slowly ripening public intelligence for music as an art on the same level as poetry, painting, and drama, which do not exist solely for public entertainment."

Embedded among his theses are brash *pensées*: "Silence plus one note can be musical, but one note is not music." "For Cage as for Stravinsky, the name 'Beethoven' symbolizes all that is lumped together in misuse of the word *genius*." "No (Jewish) composer . . . whether or not he wished such recognition, has seemed to the Jews in any country to be the musical voice of their tradition." He talks of Elliott Carter's "honest but cautious radicalism," and of Chopin as the last classicist who could not be called a neoclassicist. And he disproves the bromide that jazz is the unique contribution to American music.

Other details strike me as dubious: "A strong libretto can sustain inadequate music, but the best music cannot sustain an inadequate libretto." Or: "Poulenc's . . . guillotine offstage distracts from the music"—when precisely that guillotine *is* the music, each horrendous crunch of which precipitates a modulation. Or when he takes at face value Cage's faulty syllogism— ("Composing's one thing, performing's another, listening's a third. What can they have to do with one another?")—some may wonder at his earlier plea (and how right he is!) for "the need for good humor." Others may lift an eyebrow when Busoni, Bloch, Harry Partch, or even Lou Harrison (justifiably called "one of the most gifted melodists of this century") are scrutinized for pages, while none other than Aaron Copland is dispensed with in a paragraph.

But he does describe so well (and it can't be done!) how music *sounds*, merely by stating the methods, theoretic and practical, from which a composer—Messaien, say, or Ruggles—proceeds.

The volume represents years of realistic examination in depth. But what Yates has gained in depth he has lost in breadth: his book is too long, and by the same token too short. In a rather unfelicitous no-nonsense style (especially in the first half—in the second he sometimes attains unprecedented, if purple, perception) he reiterates aspects of favored trends while almost ignoring others. No essay can, of course, ever have the last word, but one as ambitious (and redundant) as this cannot afford only a cursory glance toward composers under fifty, and no glance at all toward those under the stigma of what he might term "tiresome conservatism." Yet despite his biases—and all valid historians are biased—Yates does not, except by his silence, come off as a judge. "To keep art in growth," says he, "we should keep it in trial—not on trial."

Around My Past

> *. . . and I shall lay up a store of entertainment for my after life. Very often we have more pleasure in reflecting on agreeable scenes that we have been in than we had from the scenes themselves.*
>
> —BOSWELL, in his early journals

> CECILY. *I keep a diary in order to enter the wonderful secrets of my life. If I didn't write them down I should probably forget all about them.*
>
> —OSCAR WILDE,
> The Importance of Being Earnest

Fiction is back, and criticism is out. That which yesterday we formed with such desperate care became a fable today. Lives are not facts.

•

Just as illegible handwriting means semiconscious bad manners, so slovenly musical calligraphy signifies a disordered composer. Not that disorder is necessarily negative, or that negative is necessarily bad. But music presumably needs to be reinterpreted, and a clean script saves money. I learned more in six months as a professional copyist than during four years at the conservatory.

•

I don't know where my music comes from or what it means. It interests me to hear others analyze their reactions to my work, though I can't identify with their identification.

•

Being in love precludes knowing about being in love. Conversely, a critic of music may often resemble the man who, never having known love, becomes a marriage counselor. Filled with sensible advice and wise dissection, he still never quite puts his interpretive finger on the exquisite malady's sore spot. Because there is no interpretation of love (though there may be successful formulae for marriage). By the same token, inasmuch as a great piece resists analysis, opinions about (even physical reactions to) it are worthless. Masterworks can't be taken apart like watchworks; what happens within them is what happens, that is all; not what a musicologist tells us happens. Meditation more than analysis will take us toward the heart of music, but to reach that heart is paradoxically to kill it.

How long does love last? as long as anything lasts—a lifetime.

Once I thought of beauty and greatness as absolutes. No longer. A Leonard Meyers may "prove" Beethoven to be greater than Debussy, yet to me Beethoven sounds outmoded. Am I not the final judge? But let's concede he's greater than Debussy—he remains less great than Ravel.

Kids today can't take Beethoven as a master because they don't think in terms of masterpieces.

A composer learns nothing about himself from thoughtfully comprehensive studies describing creative phenomena. Even Tovey and Langer end at that crucial point where the composer begins. Probably long after we've uncovered the very secret of life and the source of our universe, the puzzles of the "artistic process" will still be with us.

•

James Holmes privately suggests that I may (as is the case with amateur "stylists") be overemphasizing the mannerism of parentheses in these essays on music. Such a mannerism (adds he) is o.k. in the diary, since a diary is nothing if not parenthetical.

Parenthetically, in our America the personal journal is not, as in the France of Amiel or Martin du Gard, a standard literary expression. Especially a composer's journal. But I am shy and set a precedent: I confess on the page instead of in talk. And admit I'm as curious as the next one about where it all comes from. Music represents my order. The diary my disorder—but orderly disorder. Though perhaps all music, too, is orderly disorder.

•

Withdrawal symptoms—withdrawal from society. Thanksgiving Day (1967), it rains now, and I'm shut away, forever it would seem, imprisoned within this century. Outdoors a park, soggy and leafless. Sadness hangs over the waking life like fog on that swamp, influential yet irrelevant to the world's mistakes. Sadness pervades the dreaming life as well, a trillion-tonned heaven descending to settle ineffably here from where we don't evade, expectations overwhelmed on a hopeless map.

Everyone's depressed and thinking little on art. Small wonder: we paddle through the digestive track of this ill earth whose poison washes us always. Waste, shame, guilt, waste. All not directly contributing to work is guilt, shame, waste, guilt. Yet most of our life goes to food and high drink, society, toilets, movies, family responsibility. Can these not be classified as contributions? No. Work is work. It isn't through experience but from imagination that art is made.

•

I still place hope in nearly any passerby, wondering could you love me, do you (you do) without knowing it? I still put faith in almost every new encounter, wondering. Yet they all collapse (while I sicken with envy at lovers behind blinds) because we won't learn to adore each other's differences.

It's not that we want to be understood: we want not to be misunderstood. Nor that I have a "block," nor that I'm without ideas; I've never felt fertiler. It's that I've grown scared of the obligatory solitude of notation.

•

A note on diction. . . . The solitude of notation began early: I started to talk and to compose almost at the same time. The first music, and much of it since, was for that impure medium known as vocal; impure, because it conjoins two arts by setting words to tones. Why I was initially attracted to songs, and why that attraction continues, is unsure. Certainly I can't sing; perhaps that's the answer: composing expresses the invisible singer within us all.

The first words I set as a child were those of my own language, English. Over the years I've composed in French, Italian, Latin, even in ancient Greek. Never convincingly—though I speak and think in some of these tongues.

It was not for a long time, during the cruelties of growing up, that I realized the generalized world about me was not made up of composers like myself. Nor, for a while after that, did I realize that the particularized world of my profession was not formed of musicians writing songs in English, or even songs at all. I did learn quickly, however, that singing in English was considered, by American teachers of that time, somewhat low class. Which is one reason, albeit minor, why the art and practice of the song recital is now a dead issue. Yet the only thing bad about songs in English is bad English.

Later I learned bemusedly how many of my colleagues considered the writing of songs "difficult." Now, writing music— the doing of anything well—is difficult. Of course, song-writing is a specialty within a specialty, so some composers are drawn to it, others aren't. I'd always found word-setting to be as natural as speaking; that very naturalness, plus love of verse, drew me to song. No matter what language we are born to, we each, as individuals, speak that language in our own special manner. I set words to music as I talk them: which is what makes my songs personal—if indeed they are.

As to the diction business in the interpretation of those songs: inasmuch as I feel the settings to be natural, or rather, inevitable (for art isn't natural, it's art), I've never understood why singers aren't understood. Doubtless they're primarily concerned more with the sensual (meaning sound) than with the intellectual (meaning verse). Maybe there's also a question of embarrassment when they sing in their own tongue. For while self-expression through song is something all desire but few fulfill, interpretation of songs is more than self-expression: it is self-commitment, and hence somewhat compromising. To be put on the spot is embarrassing if we don't know what we're talking about—or singing about. So, many singers rely solely on beautiful noises to pull them through. (This is more true between the coasts than in California or New York where the preponderance of Italian and Jewish vocalists learn, through ethnic extroversion, no shame at word sense.)

Certainly I'll take the blame for blurred diction if in making a given piece—a coloratura vocalise, for instance—I decide to sacrifice sense to sensation. But mostly I conceive within a tessitura that will gratefully express the meaning of a poem—at least its meaning as I mean it.

As to my own physical reaction while listening: I am constantly torn between which is more outrageous or less satisfying: the gorgeous voice mouthing words not one of which is understandable, or the mediocre voice of absolute intelligibility. The ideal combination, a gorgeous voice with clear enunciation, even among our most respected artists, seems rare, for some strange reason. Strange at least for me. Because if the words are well set, and if the concert singer spent more time in deciding what those words connote (like the pop singer does) than in quibbling over consonants, I as a composer would think his battle three-fourths won.

•

On one side I grew up a spoiled child perhaps, but with sentiments of insufficiency—what teachers termed "a sloppy thinker." Effete yet fiercely timid, fattish (was I ugly?), unpopular with Sportsmen, esteemed by the Intelligent whom I took for granted and hence didn't in my turn esteem; uncultured, nonetheless, so raped for prettiness (was I pretty?) by those more ripe, more knowledgeable. Submerged, that is, in an insecurity which may be a prerequisite of "artistic" personalities—though certainly the inverse does not hold: so many of the insecure are drab, uncreative; and perhaps I was (may even still remain) one of them. Despite an ingrained Quakerish non-violence, has my will to be a Successful Artist coincided with a need for vengeance on those who once treated me anonymously? Could such vengeance make of me, indeed, an artist?

Oh, the conceit of the masochist! the sadist's vanity! An artist never forgets, and in remembering goes beyond limits. His treatment of history is no less misconstrued than an historian's.

•

History, or the wisdom of hindsight. If Stravinsky laments that the 75-year-old Schoenberg was denied a grant by the Guggenheim Foundation, why did Stravinsky himself not come to the master's aid? Do I, with *my* Guggenheim Grant, reprimand Stravinsky who, being Stravinsky, is right even when wrong, who belongs to a race apart? A race of one; not that undifferentiated collection of Orchestra Men, nor conductors who also form a breed apart, nor their wives, still aparter.

The Big Symphony Orchestra Player, that most skilled of musicians, is of necessity amorphous. Unlike the actor who's only too willing to be seen on stage without a fee, the Orchestra Player pertains to a benevolently fascist mass. He is absorbed, anonymous, so his trade union is strong; he speaks not of Dohnányi but of dames, cards, dough. For as everyone knows, he's a frustrated soloist. (As with the unloving marriage counselor, let's reverse the image: he never made it as an orchestra man, so he became a soloist. Or: the composer as critic *manqué*.) Conductors? They are at once doting mothers and spoiled babies, amiable, gregarious, appallingly susceptible to flattery from young ladies. Their wives long ago learned long-suffering, keeping their cool by observing you with eyes exclaiming: He may be yours now, but not for long! Yet finally their mates are faithful, having little time for indiscretion. As everyone else thinks so little on art, small wonder.

Is this legible writing unconscious bad manners? Have I lost any friends here? Unlikely.

•

Il faut être absolument moderne, said Rimbaud. And Ezra Pound said: Make it new. Ah, the tradition of the new! Yet for nearly three millennia before the "modern" era both male and female apparel remained pretty much the same: tunic and toga, comfort and grace.

MAKERS OF MANNERS

•

I made my song a coat
Covered with embroideries
Out of old mythologies
From heel to throat;
But the fools caught it,
Wore it in the world's eyes
As though they'd wrought it.
Song, let them take it,
For there's more enterprise
In walking naked.

—YEATS

I AM UNCONCERNED WITH CLOTHES, SO WON'T mention it except to mention it.

•

There is no such thing as a well-dressed artist, much less The Well-Dressed Artist: these two implied occupations cancel each other out, since both are full-time jobs.

•

By definition an artist does not dress, he undresses. His business—sometimes his pleasure—is to expose himself. Even his skin is ripped off, flung to a wind that sweeps it beyond our horizon. We then applaud a throbbing heart laid bare. The heart's blood drips to the ground. Weakened, the artist stumbles, staining his shoes. Next day red shoes are In.

What he happens to wear for this striptease is inconsequential to him, since he is not a performer (e.g.—the dancer, conductor, tragedian who will ultimately interpret his work) but a creator. Creation is a private affair. A painter at work would only soil his Brooks Brothers Shirt, if he had one to soil.

•

It's the nine-to-fivers who change shirts, keep up appearances, are seen. An artist when seen (I speak always of so-called creative artists, never of executants)—an artist when seen is no longer an artist, but a man *representing* the person who painted that picture or composed that piece. Perhaps this man is Well Dressed; but if, as people say, he is also Great, whatever he wears is right. What he wears is right if he is The One to wear it. He is the one, if elected. Who elects? A faceless consensus. (Warhol's dark glasses at midnight are *chic*.) It's not He the Artist but He the Flirt who dresses. Flirtation and the knack for clothes are both called arts, but they are not arts which here concern us.

•

Women dress to impress in this order: each other, men, themselves; but they dress to please, in this order: men, themselves, each other. Men dress to impress themselves, each other, women; and to please themselves, women, each other.

Artists—and here I distinguish them less as another sex than as another species—dress to console (or to disdain, which is the same) the public. A beard can be high fashion: Allen Ginsberg's is more emulated than Major Schwepps'—or whatever his name is. And yes, even a stance is habiliment: Glenn Gould's slouch, Corelli's chestiness, Bernstein's hip-swing. But these are performers. It is Ginsberg the actor, not the poet, who doesn't shave. Nor is it Bernstein-the-composer who once sported a

Koussevitzky-type cape, or who now employs a private tailor. Composers aren't hams: it isn't the composer within Virgil Thomson but the sometime baton-flashing socialite who is garbed by the men's store of Lanvin.

•

Lanvin's gorgeous daughter Marie-Blanche, the late Comtesse de Polignac, was a soprano of rare quality. Indeed, were I lost on a desert island with a choice of only five LP records, one would be her singing of Monteverdi's madrigals under the direction of her dear friend and mentor, Nadia Boulanger.

Marie-Blanche once told an endearing story about Mademoiselle Boulanger who, as everyone knows, is still at eighty the world's most consecrated and influential pedagogue of music. Clothes have never been among her chief concerns. Around 1930, for conductorial appearances, she ordered *chez* Lanvin a *passe-partout* unprepossessing gown of severe black, expensive but no-nonsense. As this gown was still serving her active professional purposes some twenty years later, Marie-Blanche gently offered to have a new one made. Boulanger quickly agreed, returned to Lanvin, and asked for a copy of the very same dress— which she used for many years more.

•

A Frenchman spends his last pennies on a *coup de rouge*, an Italian spends his on a necktie. That same tie on the Frenchman wouldn't work, for he's let his stomach go. Clothes may make the man, if he's raw material, but clothes won't make *a* man. Only Americans persist in believing the contrary, probably because they seldom calculate in terms of "last pennies."

•

Taste is not necessarily related to intelligence or education, or even to art. Taste is natural implicitly, art is unnatural. Fashion (which *au fond* means taste) is comfortable essentially, art is painful: the difference between play and work.

Good cooks deal in taste—literally in taste buds—but make no guarantee against upset stomachs. Good art upsets *before* being tasted; ultimately it purges us—makes us feel good. If it is to our taste. Because great art may be great, yet still not to our taste. I admire Beethoven unqualifiedly, but I don't *like* him.

A dish once tasted and swallowed disappears forever. So, perhaps, does a Delacroix, a Russian play, certainly a symphony's performance. But the cooking, unlike the painting, cannot remain in the memory. (Art concerns only two of the five senses: sight and sound. No art is devoted to touch, taste or smell.) It must be repeated forever; tongues forget. Even hearts remember falsely from one moment to the next.

Painters and composers (even poets) make good cooks because they're used to mixing colors, judging volumes. Yet their cooking resembles only the palette or score sheet; it is just a preparation.

•

LSD, if nothing else, intensifies taste (except a taste for food; food is out of the question). So the color of your socks, your sweater, had better be of genuine vegetable dye; otherwise you'll tear these clothes from yourself and go naked. Naked like the poet. (The acid test: will it hold up under LSD?)

•

"Fashion is beauty that grows ugly, art is ugliness that grows beautiful," bravely stated Madame Chanel.

Yet by a third convolution, fashion emerges from art. Because fashion is the shadow of art, expensively out of date, obtrusively in the background!

In France, always less specialized than America, one sees *les grands couturiers* along with statesmen, authors, and high-ranking policemen in private centers of culture. The *couturiers* impose this generalized culture onto their product; they rifle not from a rival *couturier* but from a painter. In America the dressmaker does not steal the painter's canvas, but the painter's very clothes off his back, absconds with the superficial, blue denim, corduroy, psychedelic patterns, and charges unthinkable prices. Like a Cheshire cat the painter himself sits back, smiles at his cheap sexy pants, then opens his own *boutique* and, to rich ladies, vends these Emperor's New Clothes.

•

It has not always been so. Look at the formal busts of Bach and Handel, their wigs and lacey cuffs; they dressed like everyone else of the period. Before the Industrial Revolution an artist pertained to his society; he set the "tone" through his work, not through his public-private style. His Bohemianism developed when he was put aside as a superfluous commodity, a luxury. When the newly emerging Business Man shortened his hair, the composer let his grow longer. Socially he contradicts.

Look then at today's formal busts: the apparel of what's called Establishment resembles a rainbow (reflecting ever-so-dimly ex-president Truman's summer shirts) and the sexes merge through their coiffures, while Copland or Milhaud or Stravinsky never go out without a tie. The Long-Hair Composer? Now the definition holds only when hairdos are switched: Mod locks are longer than Liszt's, but the "serious" composer clips his as befits the University Professor he's become.

Poet Bill Berkson is one of the world's Best-Dressed Men, so he doesn't "look like" a poet (only the non-poets of Tompkins Square look like poets). But he *is* a poet, therefore he looks like one. But therefore he isn't . . . etc. By being, he dictates involuntarily, like a king. And only the poor can afford to be well-dressed. (Poor means conformist; Afford means frightened; Well-Dressed means unmusical.)

Artists resemble royalty who, like Henry the Fifth soliciting a kiss from the recalcitrant Katharine of France, observe among themselves: "You and I cannot be confined within the weak list of a country's fashion . . . and the liberty that follows our places stops the mouth of all findfaults. We are the makers of manners."

In Memory of His Feelings

> *. . . and Ned is glad*
> *not to be up too late*
> > *for the sake of his music and his ear*
> > *where discipline finds itself singing and even screaming away*
> > > —FRANK O'HARA, *Love Poems*

13 August 1966

Here we are at Fire Island where three weekends ago Frank O'Hara was struck and destroyed, quitting this world with the same intensity that he lived in it. The need for comment lessens, time passes, and Frank left a harem of literate widows each of whom has already composed epitaphs less compelling than those he wrote for movie stars. So no need for comment, but a great need for phoning Frank to get his opinion on it all! I've reread the 8 or 10 letters he wrote to me in Europe during the fifties (none after: we grew apart once we lived in the same city) and was impressed anew not only by his intelligent humor, but by how urgently he seemed to want me to be a good composer. How many artists care, really, about their friends as artists, except for instruction? Frank, while he lasted, was the exception, until it killed him. . . . It always used to be my habit at gatherings to ask Joe LeSueur: "Who in this room will be the first to die?"

•

His poems were, among other things, conversational, elliptical. Frank died in the middle of a sentence.

•

"Oh sing us *Hôtel* again, Ned." The request was genuine, though spoken in inebriation, and referred to my notorious moans resembling a cow aborting which Frank kindly nonetheless found musically rewarding.

•

I did not choose my profession, it chose me. Since childhood it has grown between me and people. A strangling protection. My music is all one love-letter, but to whom?

Frank O'Hara knows this but reacts otherwise, calls his poem by another name: Lucky Pierre. That poem itself is gratified, being squarely between the poet and his love, instead of between two pages. And it exists, remains, can be referred to (which a phone call can't).

Yet Frank is estranged and growing more so. Because—not despite—of his art.

Strangling protection or Lucky Pierre, whatever you call art, that art takes, drains, thrives, empties us forlorn.

All's in a name. A rape by any other name would feel less good.

•

I believe in the word, even in two or three, in stringing them together. But I do not believe in writing. Not that it can't be done: it's been too much done. Ditto for notes. But simultaneous notes are more amusing than simultaneous words. Music has more potential.

•

If Winter comes can Spring be far—*behind*? But Spring's ahead and waiting. Winter overtakes, dissolves into, and is excreted by Spring. Then do seasons arrive before or after each other, or spiral about, intertwining, contradicting time?

•

So where do we go from here? To boredom. There's no beginning and end, and boredom's integral to it. Though one can vainly ponder as to how boredom, as we know it, might be a part of Eastern Art and Music. Twain don't meet.

Toward the middle of *The Chelsea Girls* I turn to Jack Larson: "It's a masterpiece, isn't it? And shall we leave now?"

•

To make a masterpiece was not Frank's pursuit. A masterpiece is for the future.

X, robust and appealing, speaks with poignance about always having found him sexy. If Frank knew that now, he'd turn over in his grave.

•

The Candide theme (Herlihy's *Midnight Cowboy*, Genet's *Quérelle de Brest*, or Southern's *Candy*, versus Britten's *Billy Budd*, Bernstein's *Candide*, or the Purdy-Albee *Malcolm*) makes good reading but bad theater. The beautiful but dumb cipher-hero plunging down a narrow path causing distress and destruction to intelligent victims—whom he ignores as victims—is inherently undramatic, being unclimactic. Meanwhile, the unlikely play *Fortune And Men's Eyes* works musically and thus works theatrically (over and above its "theme" stolen from *Haute Surveillance*). The author's quartet is composed of solos for each instrument, duets and trios for the possible combinations, and ensembles for the whole with an ingenuity all true climaxes imply and comprise.

•

> *. . . in rooms full of*
> *strangers my most tender feelings*
>   *writhe and*
> *bear the fruit of screaming.*
>   —FRANK O'HARA, For Grace

We met on John Latouche's floor, December 1952, toward the end of my first trip back to America. Sonia Orwell was then new in New York, and John gave her a party. Vast carpet, Manhattan-type wit I'd forgotten, of course piano tinkling to support divine Anita Ellis whom I'd never met either, who clutched her red satin hem and threw those closed eyes to heaven screaming *Porgy!* while the room exploded with applause that only Streisand, second hand, commands today. Today, when half those guests of John Latouche, and John Latouche, are dead.

Pushed by John Myers, Frank edged toward me, and placing the ashtray among our feet, exclaimed in that now-famous and mourned Brooklyn-Irish Ashberian whine I didn't at first take to: "You're from Paris and I think Boulez is gorgeous." He meant, as they say, well; and I was surprised that a poet then already knew Boulez' sound over here; but gorgeous seemed hardly the word, even from that poet, for that composer.

Snow, and the year was closing. I sailed to France where Bobby Fizdale suggested I write something for two voices and two pianos. What words? Why, those of his friend Frank O'Hara. So a friendship was planted over the ocean which blossomed into our "Four Dialogues," originally titled "The Quarrel Sonata."

•

Here I'd hoped to quote whole letters. It can't be done in diaries—that's for grandiose epitaphs and homages he's everywhere receiving, more than his more famous peers, Jarrell and

Delmore Schwartz. Nevertheless, from May of 1955, plucked from their generous context, come concerns about opera after witnessing my *Childhood Miracle* on Elliott Stein's libretto:

Surely we must do an opera together. Something terribly sweet and painful, maybe? . . . . In the final trio I felt you lifted the work onto a new height where the music was inspired; before that, one felt admiration for your gifts and an awareness for the facility of the setting, but was more impressed than moved. . . . The libretto worked very easily on stage, but it is not up to Elliott's other work which I admire tremendously. Not that a libretto should necessarily be a major literary production. But there are qualities of peculiar insight in his other work which would not be at all foreign to the stage and which he seems to have consciously avoided in favor of a non-dramatic gentle whimsy. . . . I feel that the audience cannot be given enough, particularly in a medium where the writer is confined by the greater importance of the musical expression. . . . Bringing your own extraordinarily sophisticated talent to bear on this subject, dealt with as sparingly as it is (it is almost a "least common denominator" of the situation), is like getting a cannon on stage and not firing it. . . . I am prejudiced by my longing to have you write the significant modern opera I feel about to happen in music. There is no social, dramatic or sensational contemporary situation you couldn't deal with in your characteristically beautiful fashion, I think, and that is true of virtually no other composer now, saving perhaps Marc [Blitzstein] who has other ideas and other gifts from the ones I'm thinking of. . . . When you think of yourself in relation to the work I imagine hearing from you (and remember this is because I love what we already have and don't mean to be overbearing or overstep the bounds of discretion between one artist and another), think of Manon and Louise and 3 Penny and Lulu. Why deal with a melting snowman when a cocktail party would be a great opportunity for great music? I don't mean to harp on modern subject matter; of course the subject counts for little or nothing sometimes. But it doesn't hurt a great gift to have a significant subject either, whether it is the liberation of Flanders or love à la Onegin. And I really believe that an artist cannot be in his best work more mild than the times. It harms the work's conviction. . . .

•

More mild than the times. . . . I do not, like Styron or Blitzstein, pretend to deal with the time's Big Issues. Yet by definition my prose and music are of, and hence concern, our day. Who can say that narcissism or the forgotten themes of romantic love are less timely, less indigenous to our health or malady?

But when Stravinsky states that "artists and 'intellectuals' can be as dangerous and foolish as professional politicians . . . about matters beyond their competence," smart Mary McCarthy concurs, but points out that artists do possess a higher intuition and are good at smelling rats.

Frank O'Hara smelled rats. And from the common rats about the house he made his poetry, as Auden had a generation earlier.

FOSS IMPROVISES

•

Each composer kills the poem he loves by setting it.
—FOSS

THE INTENSE AND DIVERSE GIFTS OF LUKAS FOSS
are no secret. For years he has been a famous composer, lecturer,
conductor, world traveler and good-will champion, most skillful
of pianists, and finally professor. Such indefatigability has now
overstepped mere self-expression and (like Foss's orderly minded
countryman Schoenberg) sought to found a school. He has fused
his talents in a practical theory whereby composer, performer
and audience presumably share the simultaneous joys of creation.

Foss explains it as "system and chance music," based on new
premises with a symbolic notation of his own contrivance. That
notation is translated into sound by the performer who "holds
the reins," correcting rather than surrendering to chance. The
rigid planning makes spontaneity feasible when an ensemble
rather than a soloist is involved. And the listener is pleased.

The composer and his excellent colleagues (particularly clarinetist Richard Dufallo) maintain that one welcomes an expression which need not presuppose immortality to claim validity—the "validity" being the fascination of ever-changing contours, risk, unrepeatability, absorption in a process wherein anything may happen any time and never again.

If the prime function and appeal of these studies* lie in unpredictability and lucky accidents which should be heard live, a recording becomes as contradictory to the *raison d'être* as a series of filmed kaleidoscope images. The Victor release by definition offers nothing unpredictable after one hearing, and must be considered solely as a static document. Nor does the composer pretend to perpetuity, wishing only to distribute his still-rough experiments, that others may develop them with more sophistication.

To judge the disk, then, is not to judge the intent. As heard here, the elements of chance and control become oil and water, neither very pure. To quote Morton Feldman (who should know), the music of chance necessarily avoids stylistic rhetoric. Rather than chancing a choice, its practitioners "choice a chance," as Lou Harrison used to say. On Foss's improvised tightrope, the risks are run over a wide net of standard compositional formulas. They emerge like unrealized doodlings from the composer's notebook, for each piece bears his stamp (or that of his past influencers) and not that of a mass personality.

The ultimate effect of the album's larger pieces is of a long-hair jam session lacking the urgency of jazz—and jazz has never needed self-justifications like those on the record's jacket. The shorter pieces have a certain initial poise: their predetermined sections all sound "right" but they too collapse when the haphazard effect disjoins the formal causes. The listener is addressed by Babel, not by an artist with well-wrought communicable ideas.

---

* *Studies in Improvisation*. Lukas Foss and the Improvisation Chamber Ensemble (Victor LM-2558, LSC-2558).

The law of averages presupposes low points for anyone as prolific as Foss (or Milhaud or Hindemith). Perhaps his experiments are more telling when incorporated into bigger "set" pieces such as the recent *Time Cycle* or Concerto. In themselves, they are smaller than the sum of their parts.

Postscript on Lukas, on Nell, and Other Musings

> . . . Most frequently the measuring of genius is still regarded as a crime.
>
> —NIETZSCHE

> Palestrina's greatness is largely a legend. . . .
>
> —ALFRED EINSTEIN

My magnanimity cannot compare to Frank O'Hara's charity. The years passed, and Frank came to write blurbs (for me, incomprehensible) on Morty Feldman. Poets comprehend musicians more than musicians each other. It's that I'm unable to turn a felicitous phrase; I mean no one ill, especially not Lukas—Lukas on whom I'll dwell more in the final chapter. Talent? He has and is it: a performer able to build a sonorous arc in a manner that will affect our bodies and minds with satisfaction. No need to define terms—terms fluctuate while the definition holds.

•

An idea in itself is not enough, it's what you do with it. Most of us don't get more than two or three new ideas annually—that's more than sufficient for our variations. Lukas' new piece after Bach, *Phorion*, is an idea utterly unready for release to the public, like tubes of rare oil in search of a canvas, or a sexy farm boy seeking urban employment. It is incomplete, not because, as he thinks, it is supposed to be, but because it is really part of a mixed media process, of which the other media don't exist.

Phorion is the Greek word for stolen goods—says Lukas. Tom Prentiss says only the plural *phoria* means stolen goods; phorion means damning evidence.

●

He used to write what singers liked to sing. Maybe they've come to like what he now writes; I wouldn't know—they no longer come my way. But Adele Addison did *Time Cycle* as though it were a master's piece; and years ago Nell Tangeman performed the little songs as though they were Schubert. And so they rather were. Though today his vitality seems conformist, he is a square dynamo.

●

It is integral to singers as (I'm told) to terminal cancer patients not to believe in their own decay, no matter how authentic evidence may be shown to the contrary. But whereas such "disbelief" is, for the sick man, self-protective (a compassionate foliage offered by God), for the singer it is arrogance purely.

●

17 November 1965

The phone woke me this morning. It was Newell Jenkins to say that our Nell was dead in Washington. She'd lain lifeless for days before the police broke into the room. . . . With sad relief I felt: so it's finally happened! And for hours now involuntarily I've been reviewing our seventeen years of on-and-off friendship. It's curious how my elephantine recall declares I've not led a life but *lives*: each overlapping strand with every friend completes its separate trip and, like muscle fiber, never joins except in a diary's blur. Nell was the first to sing my songs "big time," establishing us both as "recital dealers" in an age when the recital was through. But in examining our mutual adventures (through Town Hall, Turin, Hôtel Bisson, A.A., Denver) until her gloomy long-distance calls with an unrecognizable voice six weeks ago—was this the mezzo that launched a thousand fans? —I see that each was punctured (I meant to write punctuated) by states of emergency; states which to others might occur four or five times in a lifetime were, to her, weekly episodes. While wondering, "God, did I do all I could!" I add in fright, "There but for His grace go I!" For Nell was no longer in my life when she died. But for a time she *was* it. Today the sun is streaming through all my rooms.

•

Like *The Blood of a Poet* this diary fulfills a need no more self-exposing than Paul Goodman's best book *Five Years*. But oh the energy it takes to call off a date: keep it, *kvetch* later, repent in haste; whereas Paul complains about being stood up. . . . After my third diary is published, it and the other two on New York and Paris will represent purgatory, heaven and hell. It is not for me to divulge which is which, assuming I know.

Hellish moments however are seen through friends. Nell, after her initial triumphs with Robert Shaw and Messiaen in the late forties, and the marvelous review from Virgil, observed hell in the shape of undesired death approaching. And did not keep a diary.

She assumed the privileges but not the responsibilities of a prima donna. If she lacked the bigger-than-life presence of a Steber at a party, she did have a brazenly appealing Irish laugh— at least until the seventh martini when (eyes blurred and mouth flowing) she'd fall onto her host or hostess. But she retained too little stamina for work, too little natural voice or temperament to carry her through. It was intelligence and novel repertory that made her briefly—too briefly—an important mezzo.

Nor did she receive a single dignified obituary. Thus the performer, though represented by no matter how many dazzling disks, cannot lug his glories—as presumably composers can—past the pearly gates.

•

Lukas lugs his glories through life, through well-directed energies Nell also possessed and misused. The pearly gates of posterity are beside the point today. The young, even the middle-aged or Lukas, cannot sing their music any more—while carnage escalates in Vietnam—as if it "made a difference." For all I see, then, his talents are wisely employed, he who, like me, came of Quaker philosophers, plays the piano better than anyone, composed his *Time Cycle* while subletting my New York rooms when I was in Buffalo paving the way for his current influences in that city. Yes I see, then, his talents, of inexhaustibly juicy breadth, more talented (if talent still counts—and it does) than, say, Flanagan who's now coming up and whose qualities are elsewhere and otherwise. More than—but who am I to judge? *Echoi*, whatever my petty generalities have at times enviously implied, is a masterpiece (that word again! now, when no one cares, when care is only for *now*), and how many masterpieces can we hope for, we composers and audiences alike, during one lifetime?

FLANAGAN

•

The music he composed for The Sandbox *is so
exactly what I had hoped somebody would be able
to write that, in some funny fashion, the play,
though it is not a bad piece to begin with, turns out
to be better than it has any right to be.*

—EDWARD ALBEE

EVERY TRUE ARTIST HAS TWO FACES: ONE WE
see in the flesh, the other we see through his work. Although
sometimes the marriage of these natures appears compatible, it is
more often filled with the sound of broken dishes. William
Flanagan is not an exception—he is a true artist, and positively
schizoid.

There is, for example, no composer of my acquaintance more
articulate than he in musical discourse, as both his conversation
and perceptive journalism of a decade have proved. His comments generally contain a wholesome objectivity toward the
musical manners of his time and, in particular, an awareness of
the mechanisms which produce such trends. His critical face is
pitilessly cultured, first telescoping musical values, then micro-
scoping their cause and structure in focus.

Yet Flanagan's creative face is almost wholly sensual. He

forsakes the "intellectual" and performs *with the remotest consciousness*, which is *not* to say that he minimizes technique; simply that he cannot for the life of him see it as an end in itself. He has always composed through desire, never through duty, always written what he wanted, never what he "should," according to current academies. If Flanagan the Critic is a man of the mind, the Composer is a man of the heart. In an age when young and old alike push toward greater musical complexity, Flanagan continues to shed the extraneous. When serial music is as common as breakfast cereal and electronic objectivity all but official, Flanagan allows a subjective tonal style to persuade him. In refusing to conform to the "non-conformists," he presents himself as the most *avant* of the *avant-garde*.

It is, of course, his business to be *au courant du dernier cri*— that is how he earns a living. Yet his own music embodies nothing of the "fashionable" and (like Ravel who, with Aaron Copland, is the 20th-century musician closest to his heart) he has never been absorbed into ever-shifting stylistic quicksand. In the *Herald Tribune*, he wrote:

> Last evening was as nostalgic as it could be. For it was a program of American music composed during the forties and as such is unsullied by the turn to ostentatious complexity that was to characterize much of our music during the fifties. The agonizing reappraisal of central-European dodecaphonic technique—soon to become a howling influence among American composers—was at this time only a dubious murmur; the mass defection to the musical *récherché*—12-tone or otherwise, for better or for worse, was yet to come. . . .

Flanagan yearns here, as ever, for the more easy communicative style that ripened in America nearly twenty years ago during our cultural isolation from Europe, and which today we can re-evaluate with the blessing of hindsight. Flanagan's musical "birth" is of that time, and in growing he has remained faithful to its premise if not to the specific mannerisms of the period.

A sensual faith is doubtless what first attracted him to the intimacy of the small vocal forms, an area in which he has always felt most at home, yet to which Americans are but seldom drawn. I believe that it was in defiance of his own intellect that Flanagan favored this expression. Let him explain that predisposition:

> In Tanglewood, in 1947, I had written a batch of songs that I took very seriously. I don't recall that I had thought this bias so unusual because young composers that not-so-distant day ago were comparatively undogmatic. The concept of *laissez-faire* where musical practice and style were concerned was, with normal and healthy exception, the order of the day. The struggle for a properly contemporary musical language had been, most of us felt, the business and achievement of our immediate predecessors; that had supplied the "how" and, in so doing, had left us with the musico-syntactical wherewithal to concentrate on the "what." If my "what" was a poem, the fun of searching for and perhaps finding the special musical thing that would make it a song, none of my teachers or student colleagues thought it at all strange—or, rather, if they did they didn't say so.

Today, with a volume of symphonic and chamber works to his credit, Flanagan still thinks of music as "sung." Arrest even his orchestral music at any given turn of phrase (no matter how outlandish) and the phrase will somehow echo the singer within him. The characteristic of the phrasal "turn" will be brevity; its origin the blues. His songs (no, all of his pieces) are replete, thank heaven, with melody. But he resorts rarely to the *grande ligne*, those immediately-memorable, long-spun tunes that we associate with the Romantics. His melodic concept resembles, rather, Debussy's: the contagion is less instant but more pervasive, a serum which, once injected, lingers longer than the tone of old love. Billie Holiday (her way with a tune, not the tunes she sang) was the source and soul of Flanagan's early songs, and, more subtly and indirectly, of even his non-vocal music. By truncating the acceptable, Miss Holiday rendered banality classic. One could choose a worse teacher.

But this was hardly formal instruction so much as it was free pollen involuntarily fertilizing a young man whose sonorous tongue was French, whose first exposure to symphonic music had been by way of Hollywood and its background composers, and whose orientation had been the best popular culture of the day. How did he blend these influences?

In taking the sounds of his time by instinct, he attempted little disguise in the beginning. His harmonic speech was, therefore, that of the men to whose work he had, as a fledgling composer, first been attracted: principally Aaron Copland and David Diamond, under whose alternate tutelage he produced, among other things, a sheaf of songs that were far more than typically student affairs. Whereas their accomplishments now seem overrefined, their vocal lines remain among the most infectious of Flanagan's catalogue. Today he realizes that his "bias" of the forties *was* unusual: "As the American public begins to accept the European concept of the small, elegantly designed automobile," he wrote in the *Herald Tribune*, "our musical style-setters —the composers—have yet to come to terms with another, far older European concept: that of the 'little master.' Our writers bend ever toward the musical grand slam." Or, in the same article, "Song composers are face to face with basics. 'Form' will be dictated by the text rather than by a pre-described mold. And the song composer who denies having made subtle and personal harmonic discoveries in searching out the musical framework for a poem is probably not the genuine article—not a real song composer."

The texts for these early songs are nearly all by Americans, and their choice reveals a face of yet different complexion from either the lucid critic or the sensuous lyricist. With the exception of a handful of songs, like the delicious *A Valentine to Sherwood*

Anderson (1948, words by Gertrude Stein), Flanagan was lured by despondent verse—poems on mistrust, abandonment, death, with the solitude of male solidarity providing dubious textual relief. *The Dugout* (1946) and *Send Home My Long Strayed Eyes* (1949), texts by Sassoon and Donne, respectively, are all but unbearably somber, yet their lyric content is such that one can hear them daily without pall, while the heart bleeds for the man who once felt urged to compose them. Though the language of their composition derives much from his teachers, the syntax of Flanagan's expression *within* this language is highly personal.

He might very well have been divulging the secret that lies behind the success of these early songs when he wrote:

> The vocal line is a song's most elusive property. Its curves, its metrical pulse should be one with the rhythmic flow of the language; it should also come to the tricky terms of consonant-vowel properties. Practically anyone can be taught to write a just, accurately prosodized declamation, but the expenditure of these same considerations for a *bona fide* lyric utterance—this, in the end, is what distinguishes a song from a mere musical "setting."

Those early songs most surely are not "mere musical settings," but to this day Flanagan is not quite sure what made them tick. They were, if you wish, inspired; the beginner's luck of the relatively untrained. If his syntax was already personal, by the early fifties his musical "speech" was fast shedding its derivative overtones. A choral version of *Billy in the Darbies*, composed in the days immediately preceding 1950, represents a bridge between the gifted novice and the independent creator. It is the first of Flanagan's three large pieces on the words of Herman Melville whose sentiments in themselves seemed to embrace every nuance of hopelessness and poignant affection that so appealed to the young composer. But if their theme is a blank wall (it will become even blanker in the opera *Bartleby*), the loneliness is controlled by an intensity which by now owes little to anyone but the composer himself.

The cycle, *Time's Long Ago* (1951, six songs to poems of Melville) is the first wholly successful extended work by the maturing composer. Pain, again is the keynote. With *Time's Long Ago*, we come upon a musical texture far more sophisticated than any hitherto encountered in Flanagan's work. The favored secondary seventh and ninth chords are still in evidence, but their distributions have been altered by expanding intervals into new meanings—like Picasso's distortions through elimination of the unnecessary. The intensified tonal chromaticism, again, is new for Flanagan as, indeed, is the fresh use of the same diminished and augmented sounds that are so studiously avoided in the composer's previous works. The essentially diatonic vocal line is jagged and ever leaping out of the "home" octave. The cycle is "hard" of texture and, with that, more "dissonant" than any work in Flanagan's catalogue before or since.

These devices are furthered in the disturbing opera, *Bartleby*, an hour-long work composed over a five year period in the last decade. Again the text is Melville's, and again the choice generates a heat of desperate humiliation. In brief, the story concerns a deranged subaltern whose sole response to all requests is: "I would prefer not to." He voluntarily sequesters himself and dies of starvation. The pathetic atmosphere is solidified by Flanagan's near-flawless drama of sound. The composer has never—before or since—delivered himself of so elegant an agony in such ambitious terms. Even so, a traumatically bad instrumental performance rendered its unique hearing (two scenes in concert presentation, 1954) a fiasco both in performance and in the press. When witness to the initial collapse of a major creative gesture, one tends to discouragement. More than that, for reasons best known to himself, Flanagan withdrew from the competitive scene and for three years, like Bartleby, he "preferred not to." This purely musical seclusion engendered no new works, allowed no publicity of the old ones. With the spooky expiration of Bartleby, a part of its creator died.

But two years ago Flanagan emerged from this fallow silence, to all intents and purposes a changed man. Perhaps his engagement as a reviewer for the *Tribune,* which almost automatically reinstated him in the public swim, helped instrument the metamorphosis. At any rate, he began to regain his lost time by composing copiously on somewhat more optimistic texts, by writing articles, by organizing concerts of American vocal music, and by submitting his larger orchestral compositions to major orchestra conductors who have since been playing them thick and fast.

These orchestral compositions take us back as far as a dozen years. There are only three of them and each received its premiere last season within two months. Yet so extraordinary is their instrumental competence that the composer declared, on finally hearing them, that he would not alter a note of the scoring—this in homage to the intricate and thorough orchestral training at the hand of Copland. The first two, *A Concert Overture* (1948) and *Divertimento* (1949), are mostly gifted assimilations of what was in the air those days: the Stravinsky of *Scènes de Ballet,* perhaps a touch of Richard Strauss and Mahler and, of course, the manners of his two teachers who remained among his prime sources of supply, Copland and Diamond, both of whose catalogues he had analyzed to the bone by 1950. Still, when one recalls that even in 1949 Flanagan had only four years of compositional experience behind him, the innately adventuresome sense of the orchestra, along with the germs of the individual style that was to result in two years in *A Concert Ode* (1951), loom large.

The *Concert Ode* is a ten-minute jewel of high pathos and likely to enter the standard orchestral repertory. I know of few other pieces (Honegger's *Pastorale d'Été* is one) that can so constantly sustain the *Ode's* sensitivity of fingertips on a

broken heart. A year before the appearance of the *Ode*, Flanagan
was to complete one of the lesser items in his catalogue, a *Sonata
for Piano* (1950). Some of the Sonata's stronger elements were
salvaged and transplanted directly into the *Ode*, but the piece,
like similar work on the part of many good song writers, runs to
facile accompaniment figuration.

Flanagan's preoccupation with song has left him little time
for non-vocal chamber music. Apart from the *Piano Sonata*, he is
represented by only one other published work in this medium,
a *Chaconne* for violin and piano (1948). This work predates the
Sonata by two years and yet is much finer, no doubt because the
violin is treated as human utterance. Composed during Flanagan's study with Diamond, the work reflects more than any
other Diamond's influence on the young composer.

Still such stylistic influences all but vanish in the cycle
on A. E. Housman's *The Weeping Pleiades* (1953), set for
baritone, flute, clarinet, violin, cello and piano. This is no garland of gentle ditties but a series of virile thrusts. The cello line,
which serves as a frame at the start and finish (thus implying
true cyclic design), acts like some strange water engulfing an
island whose sole inhabitant is ultimately forced to cry out. And
cry out he does through a now-mastered way with solo
colors whose independent tensions melt into a common dynamo.
The force of this cycle is not surpassed by its composer's "come-
back" gesture, a huge number called *The Lady of Tearful Regret*
(1959) on careless verse by his close friend, the future playwright Edward Albee. A rambling cantata for two singers and
seven instruments, it resembles an oriental garden path leading
through a maze of vocal virtuosity into Flanagan's newest
"period."

Typical of this period is a calm sureness, a patient conviction
that he knows who and what he is within the present domain
of musical and extramusical chaos. This conviction is, perhaps,
not removed from tragedy, but at least the symptoms of the anti-

social storm have subsided. This resignation can be ascertained in the three new songs to poems by Howard Moss—the best of his career, taken altogether.

•

William Flanagan, the creative musician, has always remained loyal to the values that initially attracted him to the art of musical composition. And he has been able to accomplish genuine growth without need for translation into modish dialects. "I am concerned with the *sound* of music," he says. More preoccupied with sound that with lost causes, he is in quest of attractive results rather than manipulation of theory. He once told me he is quite as much gratified by the *sound* of Ethel Merman's blatant hysteria at the end of *Gypsy,* as he is by the *sound* of a novelly spaced instrumentation in Stravinsky.

On the negative side, Flanagan's preoccupation with sound has occasionally led him in a sound-for-its-own-sake direction that has perhaps limited certain works to too much of a single kind of beauty. Acidity and dramatic contrast are sometimes lacking. Sense of theatre develops solely through the hearing of one's music. If Flanagan's larger works remained unplayed until quite recently, he now has more performances per square foot than the majority of his contemporaries, and this practical lesson astounds his new textures.

For example, he had not previously been a "practical" composer (save his accompaniment to a pair of film documentaries in the forties); but today his palette has increasing contrasts as he writes with concrete ends in view. His backgrounds for solo clarinet composed for *The Sandbox* represent, for all their scantness, a venture into rich variety employing highly chromatic techniques. His recent and regular collaboration with the best singers of the country has produced a new song collection which, while retaining the enigmatic musical "rightness" of his earlier works, is more satisfyingly vocal for listener and singer alike. As for the accompaniments, their refinement is less serene.

Along with the new theatrical sense, which was instinctively manifest in *Bartleby*, Flanagan now nourishes a necessary appetite for extroversion. Much as he demonstrates a penetrating wit in society, his art has hitherto been shy of humor. A work in progress, *Notations for Large Orchestra*, promises to bring forward and integrate his native penchants and to underline the breathing vitality latent in all artists and indispensable to all art.

Whereas William Flanagan, the social man and music critic, is capable of learned dissection of the music of others, of probing the technical "why's" in current creative trends, and of encouraging students in the *conscious* gesture, he has never especially practiced what he preached. But when his poetic nature responds to what it understands as truth by avoiding formulas, insofar as it maintains honesty at the expense of rewarding concessions (is controlled, in short, by the heart instead of the head), Flanagan has always preached what he has practiced. These conflicting qualities in creative combination make him the significant figure that he now is.

Making Miss Julie

op'er·a, n. [fr. L., work, pains . . .]

—WEBSTER'S

Rabat, Morocco–August 1961

If on the outside I'm in every sense a blind musician it is because I'm internally visual; but can this make for opera? . . . Vainly working, toying at the keys, struck dumb when Aïcha the maid (who doesn't read or write, was born in the brush, ignores "western" music) enters with coffee. As though she knew I was cheating! Impossible. Yet I'm obsessed that the so-called common man may perceive the subtlest loophole in a form which he nevertheless ignores and could never appreciate. . . . *King Midas* is finished. The suite of pieces for Easy Orchestra is half done. . . . My discipline avoids the actual. Whenever I pick up a newspaper the mind wanders. On purpose? Still *Mamba's Daughters* is actual, though of the past, and the mixture at once intrigues and bores. . . . It's time to pack up and go home to America, quit the composer's obligatory isolation, start working on the libretto with Arnold, head toward that heady horror of pre-opening nerves preceded by rehearsals with soloists separately, with pianist, with chorus, never never enough, with lighters, with dressers, with orchestra. Never enough.

•

Opera is a bastard. In form it necessarily contains both the force and resultant silliness of hybridity, being above all spectacular. Today, when the mixing of media has grown so stylish, opera, except on the screen, seems contradictorily up a creek; even screened opera, inasmuch as it becomes a transplant, like *Bohème* or an adaptation like *The Medium*, is ludicrous. Internationally speaking, this decade's best music drama (Wagner's term) was *Les Parapluies de Cherbourg*, conceived expressly for movies. Really it's a soap opera whose characters, dubbed by nondescript voices, intone tunes only half distinguished and all undifferentiated: the various protagonists each sing the same kind of music. Then why best? The exceptionally personable cast offers, through song alone, those banalities which have never been convincingly singable from Monteverdi to Verdi, and manages, from Tulsa to Tokyo, to convince all audiences— *because it's in film.* The success represents an unprecedented "first," and what a potential we have: imagine now the more complex but mutely beautiful people of, say, Antonioni, expressing current distresses, gorgeous-voiced but close-lipped, back of their heads to the camera! What her built-in microphone did for portly Flagstad's obligatorily restricted monologues, the close-up will do for thin Monica Vitti's post-Freudian obsessions. Opera will not be perked up with new *kinds* of sound, but with literally new foci on the grand sounds of yore. So much for form.

Opera is a bastard in production as well. Composers, habitually hermits, become through this medium caught up in an hysterical society with primarily non-musical considerations; whereas with a symphony they're silent until the first—usually also the last—rehearsal, when it's too late (but if the piece is well-notated and the orchestra good, there's little to say), with an opera their concessions start with the first note.

Still, opera signifies for song-composers what the play does for novelists: possible major acclaim by non-specialized theater-goers. Sooner or later most composers get the bug, even those untempted by the surer-fired gaudiness of a conductor's career. So they write an opera, go through hell to get it produced and, after the awful reviews, retire for a year of no further output.

Their productions flop for one reason: workable opera depends less on ability to write gracious vocal lines than on construction of drama. Opera is theater before it is music (witness that fan, the "opera queen," who is more concerned with Callas' comportment than what she's singing). A daisy-chain of perfect arias like Chanler's *Ball of Fat* will be torn asunder in the shadow of a minimally musicked melodrama like Floyd's *Susannah*. I too learned this the hard way.

"Your songs are so lovely," they all said, "you're born for writing operas." So, in my Marrakech of 1952 I turned Elliott Stein's arrangement of a Hawthorne fable into a saccharine one-acter, *A Childhood Miracle*; and in Hyères four years later composed another one-acter, *The Robbers*, to my own Chaucerian words—a catastrophe: I got lost in what Marc Blitzstein used to call Libretto Land. These two works were conceived for small cast with small orchestra, hopefully tailored to the requirements of college performance; both were mounted a few times, and both lie now in limbo—limbo being the place where people sing exquisitely about nothing in particular.

But I wished, before giving up the ghost (a ghost never truly possessed), to compose what's called a full-length opera—though why one-acters are not deemed full length I've never understood. (I hadn't yet learned that the stage as a medium for all theater except dance was finished.) Here, then, in helpless fragments, comes the story of how I went about it.

•

New York, December 1957

Tennessee Williams seems to know all about life except how
to live it. Moreover, this could be true of all poets, good and
bad, except for the implication that the way they don't live is
the right way. So the *bon mot* only demonstrates a suburban
principle: Tennessee's laments portray him as unhappy, and
isn't unhappiness wrong? No. Anyway, he produces and gets
produced. Who needs more?

This evening he wondered if he should change *Suddenly
Last Summer* to *Music In The Twelve-Tone Scale*. "I think
'twelve-tone scale' is such a pretty term, but I don't know if it
means anything." "The term means nothing," I affirmed,
"neither in itself nor as reference to the contents of Anne
Meacham's monologue." "Well," persists Tennessee, "can't you
at least write some background music in that scale? I just love
the sound of those words."

His approach to music is not even instinctive so much as
plainly visual, or, at best, literary, associative. For instance, he
asks that Anne's entrance be accompanied by Corrida trumpets;
he *sees* what bullfights connotate aurally as connected to the
dark death of his unseen demi-hero. We tried it out musically,
but the connotation was too personal, too "poetic" to work.

Now I've sweated my tail off trying to make music that *will*
work, allowing its slashing and rearrangement by director
Machiz who then reinserts it where it wasn't intended. Why
object? Any music can be effectively juxtaposed on any scene;
but, being stronger than the word, music will alter all impulses
of the scene. So I strain to assert an esthetic—for the noble
fee of $300! (Producer John Wilson: "Ned honey, do it for
Tennessee, and think of the prestige." *Prestige!* I'm starving.)
Still, I've done it. For consolation maybe Mr. Williams will one
day grant me the sole rights. I, if anyone, can write the opera
so sorely needed.

Tomorrow, New Year's Eve, our first tryout.

March 1958

On that same tail here I sit backstage, night after night, orchestrating my symphony which Lenny Bernstein's accepted to perform next season, surrounded by these friendly venomous tragedians powdering their armpits and joking, while out there, supported by the uncanny lilt of my composition, Anne's histrionic hysterics against Hortense Alden grow so intense as to become unsheddable offstage, night after night. What am I doing here?

Desiring more than the maximum effort and concession, the minimum fee and fame habitually accorded composers of so-called incidental music, I've joined Local 802, thereby sadly to collect the legal salary of standby performer. Standbys, in theory only, must be on the spot in order to pinch-hit, though the sound is taped; co-producer Leroy, with low-budget vengeance, holds me to the letter: I must remain backstage for the run of this successful show. Probably the experience will be, as the saying goes, an experience, while I become privy to sordid intrigue through chumminess with glamorous *in person* actors— in person in dirty kimonos. Meantime, unknown to the York Theater's public, Ormandy and Mitropoulos have elsewhere just performed my pieces, while I sit here with India ink at the make-up table, symphonizing, and plotting grand opera around the trivial operatics of these vulnerable childlike comedians.

If a composer of background scores, in being overworked and underpaid by cohorts who couldn't care less about music, is low-man-on-a-totem-pole, with opera he becomes High Man— but at the price, now condescendingly inverted, of identical grubbiness.

•

In 1958, after I had composed the sound for *Suddenly Last Summer* (then co-billed with *Something Unspoken* under the comprehensive title *Garden District*), Tennessee Williams' celebrated and canny agent, Audrey Wood, took me on as her first musical client, thereby adding to her prestigious flock of theater folk a vague luster of dubious affluence. In learning one day that her own career had begun as representative to Dorothy Heyward, I told Miss Wood of my long desire to make of *Mamba's Daughters* an opera. Immediately I was introduced to Mrs. Heyward and played her some music. *But!* Yes, the sounds were lovely, yet not, well, Porgyish enough, hadn't I better visit Charleston awhile?—and who would do the book?

James Baldwin and I were off-and-on acquaintances since the fifties in Paris where we had gone to different schools together. I now found out that he too once nourished ideas for *Mamba*. Also he was anxious to meet Audrey, knowing of her enthusiasm for *Giovanni's Room* which he'd just adapted for, of all people, Marlon Brando. Naturally Jimmy and I didn't think brain to brain, he being within, and I quite outside of, this Negro melodrama. After some initial sketches he grew hard to reach by phone, became coincidentally famous, remote, vanished, and has never been heard from again.

An old friend, Arnold Weinstein, emerged in 1961 with *The Red Eye of Love* (and with his humor-filled peachy-wise Jane Romano, beloved of us all, irreplaceable in this replaceable age, who also vanished soon, killing with her a part of ourselves). I gave Arnold to Audrey, and together we librettoized—on spec —much of the *Mamba* novel. Arnold wrote lyrics, I set them, luscious Betty Allen learned them (also on spec), and we auditioned once more for Heyward and Wood. Oh, the music was indeed delightful but, well, not Gershwiny enough, and hadn't we better think in terms of Kern rather than grand opera? We revised and revamped, researched and then withered, listened to Odetta, hung around the Apollo, permitted outsiders to dictate our tone, finally to realize that if the Manhattan sixties weren't the Carolina teens, neither were we, as white folks, able to enter black skulls as the thoroughly likeable Mrs. Heyward wished us to—Mrs. Heyward, who now suggested that if Ethel Waters were no longer up to the leading role, how about Marian Anderson!

New York, November 1961

The world today's bored because scared. But instead of orgies for the end of time there's murder. Everyone's killed some. (Stalin: One death's a tragedy, ten thousand—a statistic.) Except in Morocco where one risks less now than in the streets of Paris or New York.

The doubts, on starting a new work! The greater doubts on a new collaboration. The greatest: for a deadlined commission. Everyone hopes we'll stub our toes next year; and Arnold's late success has gone to his head more than is usual with friends, i.e., he quotes his own publicity when praising his unwritten words.

Mrs. Heyward's death, says Audrey, causes complications because she never signed that to which she verbally agreed. Since I've learned that the worst is often possible, the Ford Foundation might easily go down my drain and Arnold's.

This afternoon a visit to Tom Prentiss. How good, sober, to peer through his botanical eye at the wonders of Central Park and to observe the Metropolitan's new Rembrandt which cost only $2,500,000. He advises: why not, while waiting, write *Lions* to go with my *Eagles* and *Whales*! Where is my old poem *Lions*? Who has one? Do you?

At this point Arnold and I asked about money. Julius Rudel appeared, and the chronology of even my diary gets unclear. Rudel seemed encouraging about our project and, as I recall, arranged for a bit of finance from Ford around the time Dorothy died, leaving Jenifer Heyward in charge, good natured but fickly inexperienced and desirous of more auditions. The half-written opera palled, and my interest was scrapped by the time Jenifer came through. Too late. I forsook a whole year's labor, unable any more to identify with the faraway Mamba—though her history will remain vital for someone some day with the itch.

Arnold went off to other fields, leaving me and Rudel with money but no plot.

We examined a thousand possibilities, those stacks of librettos all conductors and composers receive from precocious adolescents and crazy old maids, and lists of potential stories I'd gathered since childhood. Julius Rudel and I examined "in depth" and considered adapting into an opera all of the following:

Jane Bowles' *In the Summer House*
Genet's *Les Bonnes*
Morley's *Parnassus on Wheels*
West's *Miss Lonelyhearts*
Rechy's *City of Night*
Mann's *The Blue Angel*
Dürrenmatt's *The Visit*
Shakespeare's *Twelfth Night*
Stevenson's *Suicide Club*
Joyce's *Ulysses in Nightown*
Wharton's *Ethan Frome*
Van Vechten's *Nigger Heaven*
Millay's *Aria da Capo*
Mandiargues' *Théatre de la Mort*
Steinbeck's *Of Mice and Men*
Williams' *Camino Real*
Durrell's *Mountolive*
E.E. Cummings' *Him*
Mark Twain's *The Mysterious Stranger*

Julien Green's *Moira*
Carroll's *Alice in Wonderland*
Moravia's *Murder in the Tennis Club*
Inge's *Come Back, Little Sheba*
Capote's *Other Voices, Other Rooms*
McCullers' *Ballad of the Sad Café*
Wilde's *Nightingale and the Rose*
Wilder's *Sunset Boulevard*
Poe's *Fall of the House of Usher*
Huxley's *Devils of Loudun*
Richardson's *Dark of the Moon*
Beerbohm's *Zuleika Dobson*
Racine's *Phèdre* (Robert Lowell translation)
Laurents' *A Clearing in the Woods*
Strindberg's *Miss Julie*

and also plays and stories of Gertrude Stein, James Purdy, Ugo Betti, Thurber, Ray Bradbury, Sherwood Anderson, Hawthorne, Colette. I showed Rudel as well a series of near-finished one-acters from recent years: *For Celia* on a specially written libretto by William Weaver; *The Dying Room* on my own adaptation of Stevenson mixed up with Graham Greene; *Cain and Abel* by Paul Goodman; *The Matron of Ephesus*, another arrangement by me, of Petronius. Partly because of their shortness, none of these last was suitable. Perhaps one day I'll take them out of the trunk and orchestrate them.

•

Enter Jascha Kessler, who years before had submitted a lyric play to both me and Rudel. We re-read it. *Charade*, although a bit too close for comfort to Cocteau's *Orphée*, was the first unsolicited book I'd ever liked on the spot. Rudel concurred, procured more reassuring allowances from Ford, and I commenced what snowballed into a hundred-page correspondence with Kessler in Santa Monica about changes, levels, points of view and sound, singability, considerations of vocality which seldom occur to poets who are too fussy for song, or to dramatists who aren't fussy enough. (A libretto must be an ambulant skeleton, true literature reduced to lowest terms; the music provides flesh.)

New York, 7 February 1962

For seventeen years now I've been intermittently keeping these diaries. What will I ultimately do with them? The earlier ones are doubtless more—well—engrossing for their reportage, but the rest is mere self-exposing massacre when *au fond* I am (as Maggy says) a hard working *mensch*. (Hard working? At least this journal is not concerned with work. And today I say that work means balance without pleasure; my collaboration with Kessler and our opera for next season I anticipate with only boredom—yet what masterpieces have not sprung from even less! All this I've told in the Buffalo essays.)* The other night at one of the biweekly domestic evenings *chez moi* I read the *Cocteau Visit* extract to Morris and Virgil and everyone was impressed and said: Print it! But where? Oh, the energy I had for observative journalizing in those early fifties! But as I wrote then, we spend most of our lives repeating ourselves; so now I save time by notating telegram-style. Well, if tomorrow I died,

* *Music from Inside Out* (New York: Braziller, 1967).

I suppose there'd remain a sizable and varied catalogue. (Am I advancing? Yes, but the scenery's stationary.) And die perhaps I will, though astrologically it should have happened to our whole world three days ago, February 4th. Who'd have thought I'd live to say, "Where are the bad old days!"

•

My first taste of California's weird leisurely succulence was in the summer of '62 near my co-worker at Huntington Hartford's Foundation. During that season Kessler rewrote the book nine times, while I began and completed the piano-vocal score of our whole opera now titled *The Anniversary*, partially orchestrated it, and also composed—on the side, as it were (like a runt sucking power from its *prima donna* parent)—*Poems of Love and the Rain*, another Ford commission and a better piece.

•

New York, 7 October 1962

I loved the West, the casual friendliness of a Spanish colony with indirect lighting. Meanwhile in the East friends died: living, lively Jane Romano's quality is gone, wit forever smothered, the same hours as Marilyn Monroe. We will never see them again, nor Irving Fine, nor young Roger Nimier, while the old live on and on. But yes, the old, too: Dinesen and Cummings, and even sweet rich Arturo Lopez—or so Barbette (Barbette!) told me at a La Cienega vernissage. California is the state where you hear of deaths elsewhere, a summer state which gossips of others' winters, a place so buzzily oozing with chlorophyll, living, living, that these ironies strike fiercer. Only four clear seasons can show us how time passes. Now I am back in New York and it's cold.

•

The City Center Opera set a date for *The Anniversary*'s première (but shouldn't we now call it *The Cave?*) with Shirley

Verrett as leading lady. Doubt, queries, conferences, consterna-
tion. Bill Ball, the hoped-for director, didn't grasp the story line,
nor did our prospective designer, Ter-Arutunian, appreciate
those amateurish caverns which I with enthusiastic blindness
had fallen into, avid for fame yet ignorant of conjoint enterprise,
liking just to write notes notes notes—and could set anything,
really, to music, even the phone book. . . . Let's change the title
back to *Charade*. More meetings, reversals, rewriting, head-
scratching. Should we shelve it awhile? Try something new?
Maestro Rudel did keep the faith, and besides the Ford money
was committed to an opera from me—a *full-length* opera.

•

10 October

Dress rehearsal this afternoon of Carlisle Floyd's *Passion of
Jonathan Wade*, to be premiered tomorrow. He is an unpre-
tentious and good boy, yet how could I wish him well, since
his and mine are the only new works this winter at City
Center? At least *his* is. Mine seems to have been stillborn in
California and no one knows quite what to do with the corpse.

January 1963

Production cancelled. But Rudel has convinced the Ford
Foundation to extend my grant. So I start again *à zéro*. With
what? *Brief Encounter? Shanghai Gesture? Nightwood? The
Children's Hour?* Oh, I'm sick of opera prospects and want to
get away into other regions, away from the human voice. . . .
If I died today it would not really be—well, *incorrect*. Now, in
the shadow of forty, looking back, I've obtained the best of all
I've sought, and produced of myself (through fever, shame,
terror, dignity) an artist and a person—not perhaps to other
eyes which see shreds, but to myself at least. What remains
between this moment and my death? For though I announce
that my advancing age prefers the urgencies of pure nature to
urban ambitions, it is a lie. Where and what can I go or do

that I've not gone and done better? Henceforth I see only declined flesh inanely coupling with reason, sputtering, a dimming of commitment, a pointless ending, a silence which is not even a silence. Yet to kill myself now would be less from *not caring* as from a certain sadness which after all I suppose *is* caring.

•

Kenward Elmslie was not unknown at City Center: his two librettos for Jack Beeson, *The Sweet Bye and Bye* and *Lizzie Borden*, being visually vocal, were models of their kind; what's more, he and I had already composed in 1958 a musical comedy, *The Ticklish Acrobat* (unproduced). When I brought him back to Rudel with ideas for adapting *Chéri* we were all content.

Colette's daughter, Mademoiselle de Jouvenel, happened then to be in town. We met with her one afternoon *chez* Anita Loos who in turn was planning a straight dramatization of the same novel. But Jouvenel's representative, Ninon Tallon, threw in a monkey wrench. (The French prove fallacious our concept of American business women as hard; their female impresarios make our lacquered editresses look sweet as Red Riding Hood.) Tallon and Jouvenel were icily exigent. With annoyance and expense I forwarded to Paris unacknowledged tapes for appraisal by these unmusical ladies who smelled blood and money elsewhere.

And so Kenward, who had labored over many an original outline, dropped the project, a project with which I so closely identified, which filled me with sound, and which, since it was denied me, I would have loved to see realized by Poulenc. But he too was about to die.

With Rudel, and with sighs, we returned to scratch. Through a process of elimination by concession, and through high consideration now of Public Domain, we agreed mutually if halfheartedly on Strindberg—though only after Kenward was right-fully granted a cut of the commission. *Miss Julie* we rationalized as timely. Though not timely enough. When, then? And where? The local color of a long New Orleans weekend with Kenward proved to us that a Negro-white transposition would be, to say the least, ungainly (not to mention the tasteless quaintness of cashing in!). But while breakfasting one afternoon at Brennan's we both yelled *Hey!* how about setting it in Hollywood, Julie as big star, her invisible father transformed into cold-blooded producer with crush on John, the opportunistic extra! This would both be up-to-date and satisfy our (everybody's) obsession with movies. Moreover, each strand of Strindberg's web was transferable. Why hadn't we thought of this sooner? Zowie!

Rudel was unenthusiastic. Rudel was boss. So we kicked around other elongations, eras, places, situations—and fell back finally on the original setting.

Once again I began to write an opera, the fourth in as many years.

•

When composers write operas they usually work simultane-ously on other things, for relaxation or to make money. During the two and a half years between the inception of *Miss Julie* and her first performance, I occasionally noted in my diary cer-tain coincidental musical occupations.

New York, 3 April 1963

Overworked and underpaid again these past five weeks composing for the opportunistic *Lady of the Camellias*. Forty minutes of well-planned original music has been slaughtered, artlessly dismembered, made inaudible so as not to obliterate the Strasberg girl's babble, she whom I'm required to tutor (though it's not in the contract) in the ABC's of song. Zeffirelli is overestimated, being at best a *stylish* director: what, after all, has he ever sought out, "created," encouraged that's important or timely? What chances does he take? As for the producers: is all the piglike-agent-Broadway-bickering even vaguely near to what in the heart I hope for? At these moments I admire Paul Bowles' quick return to Araby. I swear off; but "when I awake I will seek it yet again." That boozy phrase *par contre* gave me the joy that Jennie Tourel will give next Tuesday (when after waiting 17 years she'll sing *Bedlam*), as I heard the Pinkham chorus perform my *Two Psalms and a Proverb* last month in nice Boston. Which counterbalances a composer's horrors. (P.S. Miss Strasberg could be classified as profoundly untalented.)

The play—fortunately for it, unfortunately for me—closed last week after four sorry performances. I was not asked to the opening night party. In consolation, and thanks to Schuyler Chapin, Columbia has agreed to issue, unprecedentedly, a disk of 32 of my songs. Am recording now with the five singers.

Bastille Day '63. Last night, defeated after seeing Fellini's 8½, I heard again the recorded *War Requiem* of Britten, and what after that am I but a midget! This morning in the bathroom mirror I found my first white hair. . . Another heat wave. Next week I record my music for *Color of Darkness.*

Saratoga Springs, August 1963

So here I am again at Yaddo since a week and a day ago. In default of the libretto I've been without for no less than eight months I've begun here two works, *Lions* and *Whales*, to accompany *Eagles*, in neither of which I have the remotest confidence. They're all color without content, and oh, how vastly tough are always those first days of launching into something big when not even the skeleton can yet be perceived. Without words as guide, I am, in music, not only a cheat but a loss. *The discouragement of any beginning.* Yet if I were to realize all my projects it would take two hundred years.

How I hate Berlioz! Beethoven I don't "enjoy" (i.e., need), though I appreciate his power and understand his genius;

whereas in Berlioz I cannot even objectively find what others find. Therefore, in inverse ratio to his overratedness I must deny him, as I deny Dr. Schweitzer.

28 August

This morning Leon Fleisher's recording of my *Barcarolles* finally arrived. But as though God wished to dampen these pleasures, I found in today's *Times* a spacious picture of Bill Flanagan and Edward Albee posing to announce their *Ice Age* for City Center. My heart sank in envious panic, not so much at Edward's celebrity (we're used to that) nor at Bill's overdue and official "arrival" at 40, as at the premonition that this—this *rise*, signified, for me, a descent. I've grown "to be out of fashion like an old song"—and my opera is far from announced. Yet I must continue joylessly to compose: what else can I do. Have felt unquiet the whole day.

September

Despite breaking my ankle in the bicycle crash, I've completed the large orchestral work, and several smaller things. Still Miss Julie lapses.

Program note: Twenty years ago, one morning after a dream, I wrote a poem called *Lions*. That poem is lost, but the dream remains clearly still. It opens into a room of adolescence where I discovered music, the sound of my time before that of the past. (In such a room—ignorant of Bach, Chopin, even Tchaikowsky—I used to hear recorded screams of Varèse and Milhaud, tangos of Ravel and Stravinsky, blues of Mildred Bailey and Billie Holiday.) Now that room grows vast as a cathedral, strangely cheerful, agreeably foreboding. I re-enter there, nervous, obsessed; the old blues disks are turning again. Somewhere in the night a clock strikes three. Drawn toward the closet door I open it, and behold! on the dark little floor a litter of lion cubs purrs, furry-gold and rolling. Watching them, I want to play. And do. . . . But their parents must be near! Indeed, I turn to see the male's head, great, the King framed by a sunburst halo, a desert, approaches, roars. Terror is joyous, the yellow light too much, I am swallowed, drowned in fire, in the mane, a peaceful martyr. In the howling elation I die, and dying, am aware of purrs, of blues receding, innocence dimmed, hearing the force of an obsession like motors under water miles away.

Today I reconstruct the forgotten poem in orchestration. Next year I must compose about the Sun.

•

Four years later I did indeed compose my *Sun*, but that shone long after Miss Julie had risen and set. In the Manhattan autumn of '63 I was still kept from total concentration on the opera by financial responsibilities elsewhere.

> *The Milk Train Doesn't Stop Here Anymore* adds up to little more than a sonnet's first line; but Tony Richardson seems a civilized (for an Englishman) collaborator, though what's in it for me, besides a little money, when I'd rather concentrate on a piece to be remembered when I'm. . . .

8 December 1963

I despise actors, agents, press representatives, producers, managers, directors, stage hands, and all other money-grubbing mediocrities linked with "legitimate" theater which, at best, is expensive child's play employing genuine musical talent as mere decoration. This outburst depicts relief at finally having taped the *Milk Train* score (Broadway's most distinguished music in a decade). The month-long confabs with Tony Richardson have been artistically a waste which the token fee and dubious prestige do not restore. I will never never do another play except for thrice the pay: the nervous energy and sordid interplay exhaust, it's suicide too soon, for the real end seems daily so much sooner with our Kennedy assassinated just now. Who are Tab and Tallulah up there dressed as grown-ups and acting silly? And who the hell am I, stuck off in the bleachers? Not, to be sure, the composer of *Miss Julie*.

Tennessee's output no longer interests me; or rather, it inter-

ests me only inasmuch as he wrote it (like those last pieces of
Stravinsky which interest by definition). Whereas my music
interests him only inasmuch as it's divorced from me and married to his plays (a shotgun wedding at that). Because he used
to be interested in my self; and one can't collaborate with what
makes one vulnerable, except inasmuch as people can self-
impose schizophrenia. Music disinterests him. He's said his say.
I haven't yet. *Voilà!* . . . As for Tony R.'s displeasure with the
Milk Train music, if it doesn't jibe with his preconceived direc-
torial notion, then why didn't he write it himself? If we don't
see eye to eye, or hear ear to ear, it's because I'm no maker of
hack cues but a musician with personal contributions. When
Gertrude after 90 hours of posing finally saw the portrait and
exclaimed, "I don't look like that!" Picasso replied: "That's all
right, you will." So if Tony feels the music isn't right, let him
try it, it will fit.

•

Miss Julie. The music must betray—contradict—certain
sentiments of the speech. If John states: "I lied when saying
I loved you," the music makes *this* statement a lie: he *had* been
telling the truth, he *is* in love. But one must protect oneself.
Mustn't one? That question is the drama's crux, but human
speech can clarify nothing (alas). Only art is true. Yet all art
lies. (These are human words.)

How can I go too far and still get back? Over the cliff on the
Jersey shores? No. In conversation with Miss Julie? Let's
hope so.

At the beginning of a love affair, like dogs they sniff around
for strengths and weaknesses, seeking how they can go too far
and still come back.

•

February 1964

Seen from Jersey the polluted air descends upon New York
like a giant tea cosy. I wonder today if, any more than Miss
Julie after an ample screw, I'll survive the coming summer.
Wintertime again at Yaddo. With the opera, all I can think of

is death. Approaching quickly in any form. Or formless. Am I working too well? Am I so content? Or abandoned? Snow is all over, the room is white. And I dream.

What is Julie about? Myself, carnality and dying.

The record of songs is finally issued and I'm proud. The vocalism is mostly right (non-operatic) and my piano surprises even me. While listening over and over to these 32 moods I can recall like yesterday the circumstances of each writing; since all were made *d'un souffle* I remember the weather, the heart, the country, each of those daytimes lost in the last 18 years. Elizabeth Ames paid me what supposedly is the supreme compliment by requesting that two of these songs be sung at her funeral (Spenser's "What If Some Little Pain," and Stevenson's "Requiem"). Accomplishments, though, don't elate or inspire me—they bring the end closer.

•

Kenward comes up to Saratoga for another conference. We're deep in the opera. Yet I've other commissions to fulfill, notably the Marvelous Silver Suite for Sweet Sylvia Marlowe. Called *Lovers*. Program note: Whenever I'm writing a long piece I simultaneously compose shorter ones which feed on it as pilot fish feed on a shark; they serve also as guides and diversions. Such is the partita called *Lovers* contrived in the shadow of *Miss Julie*. Subtitled "Narrative In Ten Scenes," it depicts experiences in the day of a young couple. The scenes are songs without words; events will be guessed from sonorities— sonorities chosen hopefully as pleasant contrasts (a marriage of opposites, if you will) for Sylvia Marlowe's harpsichord. I like tunes, sounds, sometimes love when it's happy and brief as this piece means to be, allowing my opera the extended sadness it must have.

•

Time for intermission. Typewriters are wearying. And the Premiere of *Miss Julie* will not come until November of 1965—

or another two hundred pages of diary. Leafing through those pages now shows to what extent a prosifying on the opera's construction did not concern me; other pieces, plus the rises and falls of love and humor, precluded writing *about* Julie while writing her. Nor do those extracts here included afford much insight beyond the general anxiety we take for granted from pregnant musicians. Most of my hours were dispassionately spent in dry discussion with Rudel or Elmslie, in clean compositional decisions, dramatic timing, endless copying and endlesser orchestration. Composers do not (like actress Anne Meacham) *become* that character on whom they bestow their flesh; if they did they'd not have the equilibrium to compose. They simply give that character the worst years of their lives. So I contradict myself.

So also the months passed then as now and always; the only difference was that Julie, being both the longest and most public of any undertaking, became the vast undifferentiated canvas on which all other activity was painted. Rudel until the last suggested alterations; the words and music were too explicative, never took off. His interference which I so resented then, I've now come to see as urgent. He did, after all, know more about operas than I, and certainly had no wish (as another composer might) to sabotage.

Meanwhile, life and love and death and meals aside, the contingent works were coming to completion. *Lovers* was done. Regina Sarfaty and I had twice tried out the *Poems of Love and the Rain*, in Madison and Muncie. And the uncommissioned *Lions* was ultimately instrumented (borrowing heavily from my own backgrounds to *Color of Darkness*), and seemed, in a sense, the most articulate of my non-vocal children—by which I mean that it left no holds barred in "inspiration" or (for me) ugliness, while being a model of order: every note of the whole crazy piece can be accounted for in terms of the exposition on the first page. My previous non-vocal works for straight orchestra had been exercises, this one was fun. Not that exercises can't be fun, and vice versa. But I had yet to hear those *Lions* perform.

(My known decorum, plus an urge for consistency, refrains, in the following paragraphs, from contingent disturbances or gossip unrelated to the opera.)

•

Summer 1964

Two or three times a year I dream anxiously of being pregnant, my belly swells with child. The anxiety lies not so much in how the child got there, or that it is there, as in how it will get out. . . Before giving birth I awaken.

I average two to three fair-sized musical works each year.

•

Virgil's best recent song is on Kenneth Koch's *Prayer to Saint Catherine*. Curiously, five years later, in my setting of Polly Hansen's *Tree of Night* there are phrases identical to those in Virgil's *Prayer*. How could he have known I was to write this music, and then plagiarize it in advance?

Ran into May Swenson on Eighth Street, looking like a newborn pixie. We've not met in two years. For 5 minutes we each breathlessly listed our recent successes, then quickly said goodbye.

Leave for Paris on the 30th.

•

Hyères. Art for me musn't be difficult, my music must come easily. It doesn't now. . . . A song cannot have padding. Opera has almost nothing but. . . . My work today? Less need for self-expression than for self-justification. There is self-expression too, of course, but with more *métier* and less earnestness than twenty years ago. Besides, what else should I do except travel those detours from death? For time stops when work starts.

Plump Lily, the concierge's daughter and hardly what you'd

call a heavy thinker, for some reason asked to borrow the record of my songs (doubtless to flatter a high tip from me later). Her sole comment: *"C'est pas mal, vous savez,* but the singers make so much noise you can't hear the music." From the mouths of babes! Now of course the singing *is* the music, but Lily's attitude is held by many a layman more involved than she. The race of Opera Queen would inversely remark that because of the music you can't concentrate on the voices, drat!

The cramped thumb aches from the eternal copying of *Miss Julie.*

Supper at the Auric's. The insect season has begun. We speak of sex and bestiality. Georges finishes off the discussion with: *Eh bien! moi, cette nuit j'ai couché avec un moustique.*

Everyone remains silent about my choice of an opera subject. The French naturally feel that Americans should musicalize only Hawthorne, Thornton Wilder, or the Marx brothers' movies. They have a point.

Marseille, chez la Comtesse Pastré. Anything—sunlight or night clubs—to keep from work. Yet this morning in one fell swoop I wrote Julie's drunken mad song for act two.

•

New York, December 1964

At Sylvia Marlowe's rehearsal Elliott Carter sits on one side of the empty hall, I on the other. We acknowledge each other with weak waves, no words, much less bravos. Next night at "the party," *même jeu:* Helen Carter does congratulate me, though Elliott addresses only Edmund Wilson (their superior minds meeting in communion) whom I'd found incommunicably tight. Next morning, the press praises E.C., strangles me. Yet his piece isn't pleasant, mine is. Which is what I mean by lack of wit. We've all been brainwashed, me too, and Casals way over there basking in sanctimonious self-righteousness.

I've simply never taken to either harpsichord or pipe organ, the one because it can't sustain (the pee-pee raindrops make mockery of Bach), the other because it sustains too much (the

pompous blur sounds like Go To Church). Obviously I'm pre-
conditioned to the pianoforte, not censoring, just taste. However, what a temptation to compose for organ *and* harpsichord
together: their separate vices would be cancelled into virtues!
With *Lovers* Sylvia's silver keyboards blend with the vibra-
phone's gold and, when cello and oboe are added, produces a
velvet homogeneity I don't need to complain about.

January 1965

Sylvia's already recorded *Lovers* for Decca. But the première
write-ups were so appalling (right for wrong reasons) that I
can only feel: we are no longer new! (we being the post avant-
garde). Don't feel like doing anything. Have only sedentary
wishes to "redeem" myself through Julie. The long days fly
past.

•

During intermission last week after the Copland-Taras fiasco
Portals (I mean, they're both so much *better*), Lenny B. tells
me he'll probably première *Lions* next season. But my excited
tears are for other concerns.

Miss Julie's done. At five this afternoon Rudel and I will
decide upon the final orchestration, and discuss singers for next
fall. So tired.

Have finished proof-corrections on *Poems of Love and the
Rain*, already two years old and technically not yet premiered.
It was an "antabuse work" written during three months' sobri-
ety proving that my best vocal music's made from silence. (The
snow-emerald color of music galleys is so satisfying one could
wish they be printed that way.)

8 April

The first spring evenings are here, wet and warm. Tomorrow
night with Regina, première of *Poems of Love and the Rain*
which Tuesday we recorded for C.R.I. . . . . 12 *April, midnight*.
The spring nights are here, dry and cold. We performed to

S.R.O. the *Rain Poems*, which were what in New York one euphemistically terms a success though nobody "understood" including the singer and myself whose heart still bleeds and I'm sad that I'm happy and nothing remains. (Ruth Ford on Regina: "I liked her less than I liked her.")

June

Bill Schuman phones. Will I accept five thousand dollars to write a piece for the Philharmonic in '67? Will I! It's to be called *Poems of Hate and the Sun* for voice & orchestra.

10 August 65, chez Tom Prentiss, Fire Island Pines

Away from city air pollution listening to various recordings of *Jeux* and observing squid eggs through a microscope. Haven't written or read a thing in four days. Sunburn. Forty-five years ago today father and mother were married.

15 August

Last night I wrote THE END on *Miss Julie*'s orchestration. It's like completing *Crime and Punishment*, like losing old friends, left at loose ends. Eighteen months work, a thousand pages, half a million neat notes. . . . Now it's delivered to Arnstein for extraction, six copyists working nights to whom (to the nights!) Boosey & Hawkes will pay five grand. (Numbers, numbers.) Then building of sets, hasty rehearsals, collision of composer with conductor, director, designer, costumer, sweat, soloists, choruses, numbers and money and time, time, all for an opening which will fail November 5th and one additional performance seven days after, fireworks and obscurity. But it's my biggest piece ever, out of my hands, and now what can I do? Write something else.

•

Order and Late Joy. Am between two works, like between day & night, *entre chien et loup*. Am looking for poems—poeming, I call it—for Carolyn Reyer's cycle, and for words about Sun for the Philharmonic commission. Guilt, that good old word. Feeling guilty about looking for poems to set to music, feeling the time should be spent in *setting* them to music. Feeling guilty about feeling guilty. Yet not feeling guilty about wasting time.

Attending a party for myself after a flop is something to avoid. Though maybe Kenward's right, maybe such parties are funerals whose arrangements must be professionally attended to. We are, after all, the survivors. . . . These are pre-opera thoughts, I feel put upon. . . . Lenny will not do *Lions* which is to be premiered instead by the Detroit Orchestra at Carnegie, just one week before *Miss Julie* opens.

September

Mass meal Sunday with Julius Katchen, the Graffman's, and hangers-on. Pianists talk of fingerings and food, and nothing else—oh, travels maybe, or anecdotes about audiences (underplaying how many people walked out on them in Singapore or somewhere because an earthquake made the chandelier a threat)—never ideas. But they are good-natured and, like singers (who speak of food only), more relaxing and less bitter than composers.

Too busy to work! It's out of the question that I compose any music for the next six weeks. Julie's rehearsals are all-demanding, plus visits to father in Beth-Israel, then Utah in a week for a week, then interviews, essays, broadcasts, alterations on the Paris Diary for Braziller. Too busy to work, but not to worry. . . .

Last night City Center gala of *The Flaming Angel*, the season's one other new production. When it was over, Copland smiled slyly at me through the crowd and said, "You're next!"

Monday, November 1st, 1965

The past month has been wonderfully tiring. If only I'd kept *A Julie Journal*, I've learned so much! The production coördination of the inexorably cold union schedule with the interpersonal heat of hate and hysterics. Everyone working for me, on my trillion little notes. The assistant director at odds with the conductor, choreographer in a blend with costumer, the three leads drowned in the chorus, the supers lost among the orchestra men who look at their watches, the management gripping the whole, and the whole pseudo-deferentially looking to me for the last word which I cannot speak. (A composer has the first word, never the last.) The climax was reached in the huge publicity of yesterday's *Tribune* and *Times* with my photograph adorning complacent interviews by Allen Hughes and John Gruen, and the cast all dressed up fit to kill. Thursday's sold-out première will come as an almost letdown. Meanwhile the Detroit Symphony with my *Lions* arrived and roared and left, mostly unheeded. (Alan Rich in the *Tribune*: "Nobody has actually proclaimed this as Ned Rorem week in New York, but somebody might just as well. Last night the Detroit Symphony Orchestra opened its Carnegie Hall concert with Mr. Rorem's latest orchestral piece, 'Lions,' and next week we will have the composer's new opera at City Center. . . . Rorem has a genuine flair for drawing sharp, striking sounds out of an orchestra, and using them in original and quite dramatic ways. There is a dazzling moment early in 'Lions' in which a brassy tone-cluster begins to expand, becoming hotter and brighter, until you almost have to shut your eyes from the glare. This is all trick stuff, of course, but it is genuinely beguiling.") No leisure for reading or writing, liquor or love, only for nursing the nervous throat obsessed with cancer, and I've had another birthday.

Nov. 4

Catastrophic dress rehearsal. Ridiculous spoken preamble by me for the invited lady Friends of City Center. Marguerite Willauer, vocal cords frozen with anticipation, merely mouthed her role, while Donald Gramm's decapitation of the bird caused laughter and had to be restaged. Question of firing the conductor (Rudel, at this late date, envisaged memorizing the score himself overnight!), but settled instead for an extra orchestra rehearsal tomorrow afternoon. Kenward and I profoundly dissatisfied with the gauche lighting. The printed libretto arrived, seething with errors. (Boosey & Hawkes has hired Joe Adamiak to design the cover; for this purpose he has bought a canary which he intends to photograph—after wringing its neck.) The fact of a lousy dress rehearsal does not—despite Broadway superstitions—indicate a glorious gala. Tuxedo back from cleaners. In twenty-four hours it will all be over except for the party.

•

CRASH! Already two and a half years ago, and I'm still not recovered. (Am writing in March 1968. Tonight, as a matter of fact, we are to attend City Center's première of Ginestera's *Bomarzo*. Maybe I'll talk of it later.) Looking back I see, scantily noted and with scarce order, the indignations and pleasures of that production.

Certain facts remain: Marguerite lost her voice, whether from fear or fever, and portrayed Julie half-spoken throughout—which few reviewers remarked! Now, professionals at cucial moments just don't lose their voices—or what makes them professional? Elsewhere we also endured misrepresentation. For instance, there was Prokofiev's *Flaming Angel* in whose lavish shadow my opera was economically given short shrift. Had I been more experienced, or more aggressive, I could have imposed righter terms; how was I to know that finished sets don't resemble maquettes? that lighters won't take last-minute advice from composers lamenting what seems a peasant cottage in cheap blackness instead of in wealthy midsummer haze? My sour grapes growing from the stage's scraggly poplar might have ripened were I less concerned with just the music. And the critics were even blinder. So, until an ideal production is one day mounted and *still* reaps bad write-ups, I'll continue to pass the buck in retrospect.

That night I received two hundred telegrams. The following

week their titillation was nullified by the nation unanimously praising the execrable production while varying in the excoriation of myself. . . .

Newsweek: "Rorem goes down fighting. . . . His melodic line flows swifly, from the atonal to the tuneful, from nervous fragments to long arias, duets and one especially lovely quartet which contrasts the loving simplicity of a passing peasant couple with the dark intricacies of the young noblewoman and her valet. The movie-star-handsome Rorem, an Indiana native, wrote his opera after an eight-year period in Morocco and Paris. 'I loved Morocco,' he said. 'Everything I've written began there. There were no diversions. The best influence for a composer is four walls. The light must come from inside. When it comes from outside the result is postcard music.' Whatever its shortcomings, Rorem's 'Miss Julie' is illuminated by the fire within." *New York Herald Tribune* (Rich): "He has done about the worst thing an operatic composer can do: to decorate a drama from without, rather than illuminating it from within. . . . Mr. Rorem is a very talented vocal composer of somewhat conservative persuasions. This means his natural thinking runs to arias and ensembles and other devices of musico-dramatic togetherness. Non-communication, or at least its depiction in music, is as far from his stylistic world as it would be from Verdi's. . . . (He makes) a terrible falsification (though) the score is of genuine quality. There are arias of compelling lyricism. The choral writing is of top rank. . . . An all-Rorem concert could be drawn from this opera, and it would establish him as a first-rate composer. He is full of ideas, and most of them are his own. But he has been defeated by context. . . . Some of the lighter music for incidental characters—notably a duet between two rustic lovers —has real charm." *New York Times* (Schonberg): "(There is) a duet of two lovers, dragged on for no particular reason except that of relief. . . . Mr. Rorem, unfortunately, has neither lyric nor dramatic impulse. He is a thorough professional, but his is the kind of eclectic musical mind that has little of its own to impart." *New York World-Telegram and Sun* (Biancolli): "Not that Ned Rorem's 'Miss Julie' is the answer to our prayers for a great American opera. Let's say it is a significant work by one of our best craftsmen, and a singable one. . . . See and hear 'Miss Julie,' by all means. With all its faults, it is one more sign that American opera is going places; if it isn't already there." *The Hudson Review* (Haggin): ". . . a futile and boring two-hour-long attempt by a man without talent to make like a composer." *New York Post* (Johnson): ". . . the work of an experienced sensitive composer, but the music is not strong enough to stand up to Strindberg." *Daily News* (Watts): ". . . yet another well made, well intentioned American opera that doesn't come off. . . . And the music never really rises to the occasion, for all the care with which it has been put together." *Journal-American* (Kastendieck): "Ned Rorem's 'Miss Julie' [is] a powerful work derived from the Strindberg play. What happened on opening night was simply that Strindberg won." *High Fidelity* (Osborne): "It is impossible not to like Rorem's melodic and rhythmic invention, the gifts that have served him so well as a song writer. (But in his opera) I am unable to discover any answer; it seems to have no point of view. . . ." *New Yorker* (Sargeant): ". . . must be written off as just another good try. . . . The workmanship of an experienced song composer is evident in several set numbers. But . . . 'Miss Julie' is not an effective opera." *Variety*: "Ned Rorem's music is the kind you 'keep hoping will turn into a melody.' That [he] deliberately avoids anything pleasing or memorable . . . is similar to a baker who prepares a rich, luscious-looking chocolate cake and flavors it with vinegar instead of sugar. . . . [The death scene] is a 15-minute singing suicide razor commercial which tries audience patience to the point where only the downcoming curtain brings welcome relief."

Time Magazine: "Ned Rorem is undoubtedly the best composer of art songs now living. 'I can put anything to music, including the encyclopedia,' he once remarked, with an engaging lack of diffidence. The Ford Foundation believed him, commissioned him to write an opera. Last week Rorem's opera had its première. The overall verdict: Rorem would have been better off with the encyclopedia—and the U.S. is still looking for its first major operatic composer. . . . Rorem, who was raised a Quaker in Chicago, spent eight years in Paris working most of the time in the 18th-century mansion of the Vicomtesse de Noailles. He returned to the U.S. in 1959, taught at the University of Buffalo. 'It was a juicy salary,' he says, 'but I hated it. Most of the students were such clods—and I was jealous of the rest.' In January he plans to accept a similar post at the University of Utah, where he hopes to create an opera for cinema. 'Utah is such a boring state,' he explains, 'I know it will be good for my work.' "

Time then quotes me as "hating" the sets. Needless to say I sent off a note to Buffalo apologizing for the out-of-context reference. But to be fair, *Time* did next week print my other letter:

> Because I do not want to bite the hand that feeds me, I'd like to amend (or at least amplify) the phrase that "Utah is a boring state." No state, by definition, is in itself boring. As for The State of Boredom, to me it is synonymous with tranquillity, *i.e.*, lack of distraction, which most artists will concur is the first requisite for getting anything done.

•

With this garland I left for Utah where I awaited lynching. Meanwhile a final performance of Julie took place (during that notorious Eastern seaboard blackout when we all got drunk on champagne) which proved in nearly every sense superior to the opening. The principles, Willauer, Gramm, and Elaine Bonazzi chewed up the dubious scenery, while Zeller's orchestra glittered and soared toward appropriate shrieks. Too late. No one came. And thus, the demi-elaborate preparations trickled away like those of the actress in *Diamond in the Sky*, like those of Balanchine's *Variants* so succinctly adumbrated by Edwin Denby, or like the taciturn *Bartleby* of Flanagan who, less grandly to be sure, expired, but no less sadly.

•

Salt Lake City, January 1966

Hard to write here now, two months later. No longer feel the need, no longer even know how. But if *I* don't write here that I can now live without writing here, who will? So I will. . . . Partly it was *Miss Julie's* failure—the publicized flop (shall I admit my heart was never in it? that I, too, never believed?) followed by the complications of leaving the heart behind and coming West. Partly also the imminent publication of these *Paris Diaries* that inhibit the hand. Doubtless my prose will receive as derogatory a press as the music—but for different reasons. (Why different? I'm saying the same thing.) Those reviewers who put me down musically, evaded the problems I was trying to solve by inventing other problems and stating how they would have solved them. The literary press will stab me for insolence, though insolent I'm not, just the diary is, and its form (at least in America) has no standard of comparison. None of them judges a work on its own terms. Nor do *I* judge, but simply, like Valéry, condemn. However, I am not a critic. My music is a diary—where no one sees the "dirty words."

•

Miss Julie, during the eighteen months of her making, never really concerned me. And during those ninety preparatory days I grew removed from *their* excitement, intrigued only by the complexities of transfer from paper notes to living breath. For nearly fifteen years I've not been concerned with what I've done. (This probably dates back to the first post-Moroccan days when I began regularly to be played, to be a "professional.") I compose because I know how. That's all. If I've anything to impart I'm unaware of it. Yet now Salt Lake offers me a salary precisely to impart what I presumably know. What I know then comes forth solely in citing friends. At least it's I who select the citations, and doesn't that grant me a certain claim to individuality? Or does it?

The archness of the preceding paragraph is exactly what I predict the critics (if there are any) will take at face value. When does a diary say what it means? The same material two hours from now would have emerged otherwise. Of course my music concerns me. Julie's failure was stunning!

•

During three weeks here I've written 27 minutes worth of music. And detest every note.

•

An author grows inclined to disdain his more successful works (they lead their own life after all) while retaining a fondness for the less appreciated ones. Maugham is said to have preferred his little known *A Gentleman in the Parlor* to *Of Human Bondage*. Cocteau used to ask, "Why don't they read my poems instead of *Les Enfants Terribles*"? And Gide maintained that the letters burned by his wife contained his greatest writing—a safe assertion since no one could prove otherwise. These opinions demonstrate more a testiness on the part of the author (he wants to be loved for himself alone, his *whole* self) than a lack of discrimination on the part of the public. The public's been trying hard but, in a sense, can't win. One is reminded of that joke about the Jewish Mother who gave her son two neckties. When next he saw her he was wearing one of them. She took a look and said, "What's the matter? You didn't like the other one?"

Everyone wants to be loved for himself alone. But what is

self alone? The rich ask to be loved for their beauty, the beautiful for their intelligence, the intelligent for their talent.

•

But where does one stop! Originally I'd planned to extract from my journal and include here every appropriate post-Julie reflection. But I've reached a climax and it's time to close. Besides, I see that my complaints edge off, dissipate, and finally vanish after a brief re-eruption in June of 1966, when the opera received a new production in, of all places, Muncie, Indiana. But of that I shall talk when, and if, another volume of my diary is published. Meanwhile a beautiful edition of *Miss Julie* has just come off the presses of Boosey & Hawkes, who will send it to the world's various opera houses, one of which may eventually present it with plenty of love and money.

Bitterness abates. I'm interested (somewhat) in opera again, even stage opera. Gavin Lambert and I have been thinking in terms of Frankenstein, not so much because psychedelia is all the rage, as because the tenderness of a non-oedipal father hang-up has never been exploited—especially today when it lurks beneath every bomb, but never bursts itself. Paul Bowles has also said he'll write me a libretto. And there's a question of making a childhood fantasy with Maurice Sendak. (My mother wonders about Sendak's having no children. But I explain—as to a child—that it's the child within himself which speaks for him.)

The all-knowing Colette ended thus one story about an old lady lamenting her young lover's disappearance: When a still older lady consolingly suggests, "Why not take another lover?" she dries her eyes and smiles. "Another lover? I never thought of that!" . . . A new-lover-as-opera can be in every manner bankrupting, and by definition a bastard who usually brings along no dowry. Yet it is tempting once more to think of reshaping another form into one's own image.

Does that image really change so very much? John Cage, in today's *Times*, with inconsistent logic suggests we need fresh food now, and asks that he not be asked to vomit up and eat again a steak he ate 10 years ago. I am no more of a petrified coprophagiac than Cage, yet I do not exclude steak from my diet of today. That diet, as always for me, consists less of words as words than of words as music. I long to return to it. So I shall stop writing here.

•

(P.S. Oh yes, *Bomarzo*. A great success. I can say no more.)

TOSCANINI

•

> . . . *but we know what men will do to public monuments. And I do not regret it. Or do I? No. I can't. Living monuments are insupportable.*
>
> —VIRGIL THOMSON

HERO-WORSHIP IS UNDISCIPLINED, MONOTONOUS, seldom instructive. What is worse, it has, in musical circles of the past century, been turned from the so-called creative and toward the interpretive, until today finally the mystique centers around the extra-musical aura of a Casals rather than the strictly musical output of a Stravinsky. It seems one does not sanctify intelligence, or even creation if the latter is contemporary. A composer may occasionally resort to sanctifying himself through none-too-widely-read volumes on esthetics. Platitudinous nostalgia, however, furnishes the much broader propaganda that deifies performers (performers who owe their very existence to the composer). The most recent book on Toscanini is no exception.*

* B.H. Haggin, *The Toscanini Musicians Knew* (New York, Horizon Press, 1967).

Inasmuch as it succeeds in its aim, it fails not only as literature (which it doesn't really claim to be) but as well-rounded documentation (which it does). The aim was to compile some seventeen taped statements by musicians who had performed under Toscanini, thus to give future generations a correct idea of that maestro's genius. Not a single composer is represented, no member of either Toscanini's general public or family, nor even anyone who apparently knew him well socially.

Five or six of the monologues are by "name" soloists of the forties; all the rest come from that special breed called "the orchestra man," one who ultimately loses his identity in the necessary dictatorship of the symphony. Neither group is known for its subtlety of appraisal (let alone literary wit), although the soloists emerge more forcefully if only because they have stronger egos than the orchestra men. These last, having borne a more or less undifferentiated relationship to the Old Man (as they call him) when he conducted the Philharmonic, or later the NBC Orchestra, tend to speak with one voice. The voice is rarely disrespectful; retrospect, of course, lowers tension and heightens sentiment: mostly the past is golden. (Toscanini, who has been dead a decade, would have been a hundred this year.) Sometimes, though, the voice splits apologetically by mentioning those notorious tantrums: some of the men felt that the constant apprehensive fear of the maestro kept them from functioning at maximum capacity, others that it caused them to function at their best.

Performers love anecdotes and are less oriented toward ideas than facts. Certain of their nearly unanimous and reiterated utterances are that the conductor had an extraordinary memory; that he was verbally inarticulate; that his rehearsals were more thrilling than his records or public concerts; that he was totally "honest" and refused to be "blinded by the glare of his own halo," especially in his desire for fidelity to a composer's intentions (though most composers aren't all that sure about their own intentions: music notation is at best approximate); that his famous clarity was achieved through stressing the linear *cantabile* rather than the vertical aspects of his art; that Cantelli, had he survived, might have been the sole deserving inheritor of Toscanini's mantle.

Everyone speaks of his dynamism, but just one person (significantly the only woman interviewed: Jennie Tourel) mentions his physical beauty, reconfirmed by the inclusion of Robert Hupka's eight close-ups. Everyone speaks of his piano playing, but just one person (Alexander Kipnis) mentions how it sounded: "definitely not the playing of a pianist." Everyone speaks of his kindness (underlings always display surprised approbation when The Great do something "human"—that is, ordinary—like showing a touch of compassion or even playing golf), but just one person, a bassoonist from foreign territory (Philadelphia), mentions that Toscanini may not have been all *that* holy—and this very dissension ("the way he demolished people") makes one examination more revealing than others.

Assuming the whole group of statements to be faithful (I don't question their sincerity), most are so interchangeable in style and content as to be dispensable. Both individually and collectively they lack contrast and climax, and ultimately illustrate little not already known.

Certainly Toscanini was an artist of uncanny ear and impeccable, if limited, taste; indeed, my adolescence was revolutionized by his version of *La Mer* which seemed correctly icy and grand and unreal, but it was Debussy and not Toscanini who provoked the revolution. Perhaps, for all I know, and as certain of his witnesses profess, he *was* a god come down to earth; but as such he was only a conducting god, and from the living composer's standpoint he was much less significant than, say, Koussevitzky or Mitropoulos. ("He wasn't in favor of my singing contemporary music: he said it's not very good for the voice."—Tourel.)

One gets the impression—though this would be hard to prove

—that many of the declarations in B. H. Haggin's book grew out of loaded questions, questions geared for favorable replies. ("Did we feel the force of his presence? Always—always!"). Haggin explains that the impetus for his anthology sprang from a friend's idea for a book to be made up of what those who had known Freud recalled of their experiences. The tone of such a book would naturally depend largely on who was interviewed. Ravel had a not unsimilar notion for a treatise on orchestration: he would base it on the one by Rimsky-Korsakov who used strictly his own music as examples, not from narcissism but because he could explain, after the fact, the *whys* of his choices and the reasons they sounded good. Ravel however planned to use only those portions of his own music where intention had failed. He never wrote the book (how could he have? I ask worshipfully), but such an essay superimposed on Rimsky's could have been invaluable.

By the same token a series of comments by cultured non-executant musicians—composers and musicologists—whose acquaintance with Toscanini was as thorough but less abject than so many of those included here, might combine to form a more instructive document. Meanwhile the title, because incomplete, is misleading. And the content, because redundant and one-sided, is boring.

A Sermon*

> If a man finds that the cadences of an Apache war-
> dance come nearest to his soul, let him assimilate
> whatever he finds highest of the Indian ideal so
> that he can use it with the cadences, paint his house
> with them, make them a part of his prayer-book.
> —CHARLES IVES

This will be short, for brevity is next to godliness. And sermons—
any speeches—are hard without an exchange. Since randomness
is as untrustworthy in talk as in music, I'll present a few un-
answered questions formed as variations on the theme of musico-
religious autobiography.

Brought up a Quaker, meaning in silence, I needed noise. So
I became a composer. The texts for my first vocal works were
chosen from the Old Testament, not because I was a believer
but because the poetry was good. (The shepherd David had,
after all, conceived those psalms in song.) But from thirteen to
thirty-five I gradually forsook the Bible for Sappho and Chaucer,
approached Shakespeare and Herrick, advanced through Jonson
and Byron toward Hopkins and Hardy, and finally ended up
at home. Home was in the American language as written by

---

* An improvised talk on Religious Music Today, delivered in conjunc-
tion with a program of all-Rorem songs performed by soprano Adele
Addison, accompanied by the composer and by a string-quartet of Julliard
students, at Spencer Memorial Church in Brooklyn, where the Reverend
William Glenesk was our heavenly host on December 10, 1967.

E.E. Cummings and Paul Goodman, by Theodore Roethke and Howard Moss, or by "today's generation," my friends Frank O'Hara, Kenneth Koch, Kenneth Pitchford, Kenward Elmslie. Occasionally in a pinch or a hurry I'll revert to the Psalms: they're good for a tune, though my heart's seldom there any more. Not that tune and heart need be mutually inclusive; on the contrary, "inspiration" is the direct cause of our vulgarest church music.

Now it's rumored God is dead. Long live God! The poems of this time, however they're sliced, are for my time, however I'm sliced, though I'm called behind the time; yet who, by that, can prove I'm not instead ahead? Despite or because of God's death American churches now commission vociferously, even Catholics, who want vernacular masses. Though I no longer feel the call, I heed the call, remunerative deadlines having always been (as all composers will tell you) the palpable inspiration *par excellence.*

Adele Addison and I still wished to concoct a traditionally "sacred" program. However, as menus aren't cooking (though they're quite important), so programming isn't performance (though it's quite important). To select a balanced meal we sifted through my hundreds of so-called godly works of the past. Suddenly they didn't contain—well—much *variety.* There and then I knew that music is religious if the composer says so, or if the public (that is, the audience or participants) decide so.

What is religion? Something communal? Not necessarily. Is religion just in words or title, or in music itself? Though it may inspire a Bach or a Michelangelo, is the result thus intrinsically religious? Are we converted to music as we once were to faith? If so, can that music change us for the better as religion presumably can?

God dead? Yet there are specifically big and important and definitely holy works being made in our age: Poulenc's *Dialogues,* Penderecki's *St. Luke's Passion,* Britten's *War Requiem,*

Stravinsky's *Canticles*, and nearly everything of Messaien whose output Stravinsky has described as "a crucifix of sugar," while Virgil Thomson once termed it as "destined at once to open up the heavens and bring down the house." But not only is this music all by non-Americans mostly old enough to recall the good old days of God, it is also all *vocal* and mostly interspersed with elements of today—through texts and/or effects. Who can claim that these works are more religious than, say, Poulenc's non-vocal chamber music, Penderecki's *Hiroshima Threnody*, Britten's *Cello Symphony*, Stravinsky's *Agon*, Messaien's *Turangalîla*? Or, for that matter, the Beatles' *Day in the Life*, or these nature poems of Roethke we're about to perform?

As for the public, the two non-operatic "masterpieces" they've hailed in the last decade are the aforementioned choral machines of Penderecki and Britten. Yet that same public buys Biggs' records more than ever, not because the organ brings back their churchly childhood, but because it provides psychedelic sounds to show off their stereophonic equipment.

•

P.S. Virgil, when informed next day by Morris Golde that I had delivered this talk, retorted: "Nothing could be more correct than that Ned, as one who has publicly confessed, should now give sermons. Churches love sinners—it's their business."

THE AMERICAN
COMPOSER SPEAKS

•

*I was fool enough to commence author before I
really understood either tune, time, or concord.*
— WILLIAM BILLINGS

*How far can the composer be held accountable? . . .
after all is said and sung. . . .*
— CHARLES IVES

EVERYONE KNOWS THAT AMERICAN COMPOSERS
today are verbally articulate, but it may come as a surprise to
learn that they were already articulate—that they even existed—
two centuries ago. Gilbert Chase* illustrates the point in his com-
pilation of thirty essays by as many composers, from William
Billings in 1770 to Earle Brown in 1963. The intervening styles
are as diverse as the contributing personalities, and a chronologi-
cal perusal is nearly as entertaining as a survey of the short story.
Nearly. The concerns, being all in the same key, become a bit
tedious. Artists' personal obsessions seem invariable despite social
advancement or cultural upheaval, and those obsessions (expressed with charm or rancor) center on the need to define

* Gilbert Chase, ed., *The American Composer Speaks* (Louisiana State
University Press, 1966).

American music, to put down the rival camp, to bridge the artist-public gulf, and to bemoan the lack of just rewards for their labor. Chase's role is not that of referee but of host. Carefully he introduces each participant and situates the circumstances of all the selections. Many of the latter are necessarily superficial, being extracts from more comprehensive works; others toward the end were specifically requested for this volume, and present thorough views on aspects of the current musical scene.

Now the current musical scene is almost as fluctuating as that of painting, whose generation's time-span has shrunk to about four days. Which is one reason why those articles written since the last war seem more old-fashioned than those of the 18th century. Also, with few exceptions, 20th-century musicians have a less memorable literary tone than their predecessors, though most are clear and unsentimental in their opinions.

With a style that is sheer joy to read, William Billings speaks of compositional rules: "Nature is the best Dictator. . . . Art is subservient to Genius, for Fancy goes first. . . . I think it is best for every Composer to be his own Carver." His prose is suave yet artless, while his music was rough-hewn as an old church door. The same holds for Francis Hopkinson, whose beguiling and opportunistic Dedication to His Excellency George Washington is included. One wonders if that president's reaction was closer to Queen Bess or to Lyndon Johnson. But one no longer need speculate when, a few years later, John Hewett details an agonizing visit to the White House of President Tyler.

Stephen Foster was the hit-songster of his time, yet then as now the money went to interpreters, leaving the composer without even the benefit of a performing-rights fee. Such pre-ASCAP troubles are shown poignantly in Foster's letters: "I find I cannot write at all unless I write for public approbation and get credit for what I write." He lamented that his "style of music [was] so cried down by opera mongers," yet naively asserted "this song is certain to become popular as I have taken great pains with it." Louis Gottschalk, Foster's contemporary, resolved the financial problem by becoming his own performer, and as such was something of an international Liberace. He complained that his homeland was the last to recognize his talents, for as he modestly states: "I was the *first* American pianist." But his writings are never glib, usually elegant, sometimes penetrating precursors of Susanne Langer: "Music is a psycho-physical phenomenon (which begins where words leave off). . . . We discover in its general character an agreement with our physical state . . ." and he goes on to explode the fallacy that music may possess specific literary connotations.

MacDowell, once hailed as *the* Great American Composer, was also something of a psychologist: ". . . to recognize the existence of decidedly unpleasant music . . . would be the first step toward a proper appreciation. . . ." His esthetic stressed form above what he termed sensuousness, although in practice his composition was by definition sensuous, since it was intensely German—although he thought of it as American. Yet like his forbears he was unable satisfactorily to define the term, not realizing that Americanism is an attitude and not a formula. (The best definition probably comes from Virgil Thomson some fifty years later: "The way to write American music is simple. All you have to do is to be an American and then write any kind of music you wish.")

In opposition to MacDowell, Arthur Farwell (who wrote in 1903 but died as recently as 1951) sympathized with the French and suggested we submit more to their influence. Which of course we finally did. He nonetheless felt we already had a distinguishing signature and all that American composition needed was publicity. Which of course we finally got. His colleague Henry Gilbert was less optimistic. In an article dated 1915 he gives an *aperçu* of the artist's economy; though stylistically clumsy and redundant it could have been written in our days.

Our days, psychologically speaking, actually predated Gilbert and began with Ives. The latter's Epilogue from *Essays Before a Sonata* (1920) is a model of spirited English, depicting the creative procedure once and for all.

From there we are led, by way of the reactionary Daniel Mason (the Jewish influence in American music is a "menace to artistic integrity"), through the progressive Henry Cowell ("Contemporary music makes almost universal use of materials formerly considered unusable"), the likeably innocent Gershwin ("If music ever became machine-made . . . it would cease to be art"), the knowledgeably pompous Roy Harris ("Our sense of rhythm is less symmetrical than the European. . . . America waits calmly between the Pacific and the Atlantic while the tide of the Mississippi rises and falls with the seasons"), and even the rustic Jelly Roll Morton ("You got to be able to come down in order to go up")—to the recent crop of not-so-young iconoclasts.

Of these last I find John Cage's habitual intelligence about all things sonorous, and Harry Partch's witty concern for human speech values, particularly far-seeing and literate. By contrast Arthur Berger's words on the Stravinsky school seem no longer cogent, and Gunther Schuller's on jazz (1956) appear by their very "timeliness" out of date. As for Milton Babbitt, he not surprisingly gives the impression that whoever doesn't think as he does doesn't exist. But quite surprisingly, he illogically equates music with mathematics by suggesting that a concert audience should be as formally equipped as an audience at a lecture about advanced mathematics, as if science weren't a means to an end and art an end in itself. They all speak of progress, of evolution, as though these terms were more inevitably applicable to a healthy musical growth than to a cancer.

"One of the present problems among musicians is that of keeping abreast of the time," declared Elliott Carter in 1958, and the point was proved when William Flanagan the same year maintained that opera was all the rage among younger composers. It isn't now.

To Roger Sessions perhaps one must allow the last word, since his thesis is the least ax-grinding, the most inclusive. He offers a rundown on every current trend in this country's music, and while praising the vitality he points out the dangers of the *embarras de richesses* now available to the young. Best of all he dispels the misconception that "a period in which musicians think and talk so much about art must necessarily be a sterile one." Composers, good and bad, have always done a lot of talking, good and bad. The present volume is a perfect example.

At the White House

> The Kennedys accompany us to the door and wait
> with us fifteen minutes until a White House car
> appears. They are warm, gracious, and totally dis-
> arming.
> > I.S., in the car: "Nice kids."
> > > —IGOR STRAVINSKY and ROBERT CRAFT,
> > > Dialogues and a Diary

> Well, I am interested in the glories of art and
> architecture and the finer things of life and edu-
> cation, but I am also interested in income taxes,
> because that is what we use to pay for these things.
> > —L.B.J.

June 1965

Against the better judgment of my mother who wished that I,
like Robert Lowell, had taken an open stand against Vietnam,
I accepted the gold engraved invitation to Washington on the
14th of this month.

Of the 400 guests at the Festival of Arts—a first gesture of
this kind by our current administration—I was, quaintly enough,
the only long-hair composer. (Hugo Weisgall represented the
American Music Center.) The 13-hour day began at ten. I
walked to the White House from the Carlton, weather paradisia-
cal, my pretty invitation relinquished to the first of a thousand
white-garbed aides, and I was instantly struck by the two im-

pressions that remained all day: 1) Who were all these intimidated celebrities? If it weren't for badges reading Saul Bellow, or Dwight Macdonald (who, as self-proclaimed "black fairy," was, perhaps tastelessly, rather vainly—the occasion being ill-chosen—soliciting signatures for an anti-war petition), etc., it would have seemed a convention of classy salesmen. Of course, artists are no more physically beguiling than "real people"; but, as we shall see, few artists were present. 2) How unostentatiously clean, the White House, with its neat unobtrusive flower arrangements, its groups of military crew-cuts performing chamber music in corners! Wealth in Europe is luxury, in America it's order. Both countries' gardener and maid are beyond *my* pocketbook.

Mrs. Johnson, the First Lady (this nomenclature was the sole bow to formality) greeted us individually in southern tones beneath a barrage of flash bulbs. Faithfully she smiled all day, disappearing only at five to change from dark blue print into pale blue sequins. She's younger, prettier than her pictures.

In the East Room she first introduced the writers who read for an hour, and only Hersey caused a stir, handsomely, in a no-nonsense reference to "wars have a way of getting out of hand," quoted by noon in Washington headlines.

Then we had 45 minutes to "view" the pictures (Rivers, Jasper Johns, Wyeth, Man Ray; no one was screened either politically or carnally).

The buses deposited us on a red carpet before the presidential entry to the National Gallery where we lunched: a so-so chicken in jellied cream, cold asparagus, salad, strawberry meringue. At my table: Phyllis McGinley who spoke only of her *Time* cover story, Mrs. Roger Stevens, and the head of the Smithsonian Institute, a Mr. Ripley who was unable to answer my perhaps ingenuous question about implosion (does it make a noise?). A long, wise speech by George Kennan.

Return *en masse* to the White House State Dining Room

where Marian Anderson tonelessly introduced Roberta Peters and praised American music (making no mention of myself, or of any composer) and the Louisville Orchestra then played my *Eleven Studies* (cut version). On my right sat the president of the Indianapolis Symphony, who talked to me all during the music; to his right, the First Lady in meditation; on my left, Catherine Drinker Bowen scribbling notes on how divine my piece sounded; to her left, George Kennan. And me, heart pounding, because the presumable cream of U.S. culture was obliged to presumable silence for twenty minutes by my presumable music. . . . Concert over. Kennan leaned across Mrs. Bowen to congratulate me, receptivity well marked upon his sad intelligent features.

Mass removal to Ball Room for the Art of the Stage introduced by lovable little Helen Hayes (holding back the tears). . . . Plays over. Mass removal to the movies presided over by Charlton Heston whom I'd not seen since our work together on Iris Tree's comedy in 1948. (He didn't seem to remember). . . . Movies over. Gene Kelly spoke of choreographing my piece, showing he'd really listened, really heard (which is true of one in three hundred), while screen directors Zinnemann and Wyler praised me (genuinely or not), doing wonders for my ego.

But now I was (and am) bored, my contribution having come and gone. Five o'clock. The schedule allowed us, like grammar school inmates, two hours of recreation, again to *view* the paintings. I considered leaving since I missed New York already, but decided to fly back on the nine o'clock shuttle, since after all. . . .

Tour of grounds. Giddy sculpture on Protestant lawns. At 7:00, cocktails. No one drunk. (I shuddered at the thought of an Oscar Dominguez there then, surrealistically goosing the First Lady's secretary or disrobing among the saxophones. Aren't artists supposed to drink?)

We now found ourselves seated on hard-benched rows amongst the roses, where promptly at 7:30 our President appeared and spoke for ten intelligible minutes, then descended into the throng and (do my eyes deceive me?) was assailed by autograph seekers. "What are we doing here?" some of us asked, as he shook our hands without seeing our eyes.

The evening buffet, consumed beneath lantern light, consisted of shrimp creole, roast beef, mushroom salad, champagne. To my right sat the Kansas City Symphony's president. I remarked: "Virgil Thomson is from your town." "Ah yes? And what's his line?" This exchange illustrates the tone of the day. Whereupon I departed for Manhattan, missing only the Joffrey ballets and Duke Ellington who, it's said, played far into the night (which Kenward, when I told him about it by phone, heard as: foreign to the night).

•

Postscript. Paul Hume, as always, granted me a pretty review. . . . Next day a gleam of joy. In the Museum of the City of New York I arrived on the second floor landing at the moment a 5-year-old nymphet in slate-blue dotted-swiss emerged from between two glass cases filled with pewter, and flashed me a grin brighter than the sky through that dark window behind her.

LAST THOUGHTS ON
THE BEATLES

•

We'll be over soon they said.
Now they've lost themselves instead.
—GEORGE HARRISON

THE FRENCH HAVE SAID AMERICA IS THE ONLY country in history that passed from barbarism to decadence without an intervening civilization. One could appraise the Beatles with a twist on that *bon mot*: they are the only autonomous musical entity of this generation to have passed from barbarism through decadence and ended up within another civilization.

Barbarism, in my definition, means health as expressed through the needs of childliness. All artists are children, and inasmuch as they grow up (i.e., intellectualize themselves) they cease to be artists. The first Beatles songs represent a violent physical reaction to those sophisticated cerebrations of the largely non-vocal non-danceable music, both jazz and "serious," of the fifties. Their sound (let us forget their lyrics for the moment) excited the body more than the mind for the first time since the war, and corporal stimulation was always music's function. This function they re-established by the most ancient and simplest of fashions: by giving us tunes well-wrought and instantly memorable—the tunes of spontaneous aborigines—though as yet unstamped with their now-quickly-recognizable individuality.

Decadence, as I understand the term, is the appeal of corruption, an attracting emergence from the beginnings of decay: in a word, art, art which achieves its highest pinnacle on the eve of an essentially non-artistic organization's downfall. For, as we know, art does not nourish or even instruct; it reflects. Therefore, by definition, art comes at the end, to oppose, as in a mirror. When art grows too ornamental—that is, too self-imitative or unrelated to the outside—it also suffers the decay it has reflected, and putrifies in its turn. Inasmuch as decadence, then, possesses non-negative connotations, the second of the Beatles' "phases," as represented by *Rubber Soul, Revolver,* and *Sgt. Pepper,* is decadent. These recordings have been so often shown, by literary critics, as climactic in our world's culture, both sociological and artistic, that they require little re-emphasis here. But they depict the group at the height of its originality.

Civilization, to my way of thinking, implies boredom. It is a phenomenon which does not precede, but which *succeeds* decadence, which occurs, so to speak, after the fall, and which signifies a torturous rebuilding that must of necessity forego the healthy abandon of both barbarism and decadence. Ironic and contradictory though this may seem, the *Magical Mystery Tour* lacks both mystery and magic and becomes a tour back to the tameness of civilization, a civilization where adults unconvincingly play at being children.

•

When I call the Beatles "an autonomous musical entity" I mean that, like Stravinsky, they are a self-contained creative unit. (I am less concerned with them here as performers—or, at best, must classify them as composer-performers, since that reconciliation seems to be the mode today.) When I speak of their "phases" I mean that, like Stravinsky, they have already gone through periods distant enough to be judged with retrospect. Yet when I mention "this generation" I mean less the literal span between the birth of parents and the birth of their offspring, than the current psychological span of an art craze—about four years. The present generation is therefore the one which has revived sheer fun as opposed, say, to Susan Sontag's already vanishing *new art* which she maintained "precludes pleasure in the familiar sense— the pleasure of a melody that one can hum after leaving the concert hall."

So much for definitions.

•

Only five of the eleven songs on the Beatles' new album are new. Two of the others, "Penny Lane" and "Strawberry Fields Forever," pre-date the famous *Sgt. Pepper* release, and each is a Schubertian gem of highest polish. The four remaining pieces were issued as singles over the past months; two of these sound like postscripts: their mood is the same as, but their quality is lower than, the colorful message of *Sgt. Pepper*. "Baby You're a Rich Man" has a contagiously clever melody and quite funny words. But "All You Need Is Love" is pretentious without charm: the preface in "bold" seven-four meter, the interpolations of "La Marseillaise" and "Greensleeves," the superfluous cute ending (like that of "Strawberry Fields" which almost cancels out, or at least apologizes for, the genuine expressivity which precedes it, just as the iconoclastic French composers of the twenties would ruin perfectly straightforward pieces with campy nose-thumbing swirls at the finish)—such devices which are all too transparent, one finds analyzed by presumably intelligent reviewers for their Deeper Meaning.

The other two singles foreshadow the substance of the latest songs. "Hello Goodbye" is both corny and tiresome; corny because it uses old-hat harmonies (in this case the Neapolitan Sixth) with no unusual point of view, tiresome because of its self-confident insistence on a bad tune as though it were good. "I Am the Walrus" is classier, and has even become something of a hit on juke boxes. Musically, however, it is built from watered-down Old English modality, given a "beat," drenched in exotic orchestration, and passed off as New. As for the words, I await their interpretation in our learned reviews. Certainly they have convoluted "In" references (to "Lucy in the Sky," for example). Mostly they are whimsical in Lewis Carroll style, and quite serviceable to the needs of song, being syllables which impel the voice to rise and fall. If, however, they contain a philosophy of today's despair, this intention escapes me. But then, of course, I'm over thirty. (Parenthetically, I often wonder if John Lennon smiles bemusedly at the serious diagnoses of his verse. It's always seemed to me that it is the critics who think of a "meaning," then write it down. The poet writes "it" down, then thinks of a meaning. The *meanings* written down by critics are usually drawn from the poets who, if they were to read the multi-convoluted ramifications credited to their works, would turn over in their already unquiet graves. The most recent grave is that pictured on the *Sgt. Pepper* album cover, a rictus amazed at the wise essays "interpreting" it.)

•

The album cover of *Magical Mystery Tour* pictures the young musicians in fantastical garb, one nice walrus and three less identifiable furry creatures. Inside is a 24-page "full color picture book" containing stills from their forthcoming television extravaganza, and a series of comic strips narrating the (I guess) story of the film. Of the film's five new songs the least interesting (the most "civilized") is that title tune, a de-energized replica of *Sgt. Pepper*'s title tune. In both, the singers impersonate fairground barkers seducing us with their delicious cockney into new dimensions of adventure. But while we might be tempted by "The Lonely Hearts Club Band," whose words and music are poignant and witty, the "Mystery Tour" declaims a tune of slight character set to rhymes as trite as Cook's Travel Service ("I've got an invitation/To make a reservation").

"The Fool on the Hill," if we want to make comparisons (and who doesn't), corresponds to the previous collection's "She's Leaving Home," or to the still earlier "Eleanor Rigby." Meaning that an exquisite melody—called "ballad" in pop parlance—illustrates bittersweet words with moral overtones. In this case the subject matter (as with "Michelle") is less narrational, more situational: unlike the other two songs this one describes a state of mind rather than a state of body. The Fool is the misunderstood Poet, unloved and dull on the surface, sensitive and philosophic at heart, like the idiot in *Boris Godunov*. The melody arches upward with gentle grace, and the interludes come sweetly garlanded with an icing of flutes and recorders. Yet despite the pleasant taste a certain willfulness keeps the piece from digestibility, as though McCartney, in deciding to go himself one better in nostalgia, self-consciously goes himself one worse.

By the same token "Your Mother Should Know," in emulating "When I'm Sixty-Four," fails. As for "Flying," this is not, properly speaking, a song so much as a *Romance sans Paroles* in the Mendelssohnian sense, which still does not render it interesting as to texture, style, or content.

"Blue Jay Way" however is not only the album's finest offering, it's George Harrison's best song by far. Reduced to lowest terms Harrison's tunes have hitherto been well-shaped and lovely as most of the other utterly Western tunes of the group. But I always longed to hear a non-Hindu tailoring intoned by maybe Sarah Vaughan. My own childhood goes back to the thirties when Victor released the music of Shan Kar's troup, a music which spellbound us long before Zen and acid were toyed with.

Yet how did we *hear* it? surely not with Indian ears! Nor were there words. Yet it spoke. But is there a point in attempting to translate such speech? No. And now with "Blue Jay Way" Harrison seems to have renounced such attempts at translation, which is certainly the wisest thing he may have learned from the foxy Maharishi.

If, as I declared earlier, "Hello Goodbye" employs old-hat harmonies with no special viewpoint, "Blue Jay Way" employs such harmonies with an astonishing freshness. In the 1820's Weber's use of the diminished triad sent chills up the spine; by 1900 that use had grown laughably hackneyed. Who would believe that today a composer could take that old triad to design a vocal line of such uncomplicated subtlety that it not only "works," but works in the same freezing manner as it worked a century ago? Of the five novelties, then, this one alone (though it's certainly no "Day in the Life") makes the whole album worth the price.

•

Newness *per se* has never been the basis—or even especially an ingredient—of the Beatles' work. On the contrary, they have revitalized music's basics (harmony, counterpoint, rhythm, melody) by using them again in the simplest manner, a manner directed away from intellectualism and toward the heart. The intelligentsia, what's more (except specialists), now eschews the "modern music concert," only too glad to embrace the Beatles instead, to react, have fun, cry a little, get scared. The Beatles' instrumentation may superficially sound far out, but apes the flashier elements of electronic backgrounds no more "advanced" than the echo-chamber sound tracks of 1930's horror movies. Their "newest" thing is probably a kind of prosodic liberty; their rendition—their *realization*—often sounds contrary to the verses' predictable look on paper. Yet even at that, are they much different from our definitive song-writers of the past? from Purcell,

say, or Debussy? It is not in their difference but in their betterness that their superiority lies.

But their betterness is not always apparent. Again, like
Stravinsky, they are already classifiable with retrospective periods. Inasmuch as they try to surpass or even consciously to
redefine themselves with each period, they fail, as they mostly
have with their Magical Mystery Tour. This isn't surprising
with persons so public and hence so vulnerable. But where, from
this almost complacent "civilization," can they go from here?

Well, where does any artist go? Merely on. Still, it should now
be clear that they are not the sum of their parts, but four distinct
entities. Paul, I guess, is a genius with tunes; though what,
finally, is genius without training? John, it seems, is no less
clever than Joyce; though where, ultimately, can that lead,
when he is no *more* clever? George, they say, has brought East
to West; but what, really, can that prove, when even Kipling
realized it's not the twain of deeds but of concepts which never
seem to meet? And Ringo, to at least one taste, is cute as a bug;
though anyone, actually, can learn quick to play percussion, as
our own George Plimpton now is demonstrating.

We've become so hung up on what they Mean, we can no
longer hear what they're performing. Nor was Beethoven ever so
Freudianized.

Just as twenty years ago one found oneself reading more
books about Kafka than reading Kafka himself, so today one gets
embarrassed at being overheard in deep discussion of the Beatles.
I love them. But I love them not as "symbolic layers" of The
Scene (or whatever it's called), and even less as caricatures of
themselves (which, like Mae West, they're inclined to become).
I love them as the hearty barbaric troubadours they essentially
are. As such I hope they will continue to develop, together or
apart, for they represent the most invigorating music of an era
so civilized that it risks extinction less from fallout than from
boredom.

More Random Notes

If I play an F in a tune called Peace *I don't think it should sound the same as an F that is supposed to express sadness.*

—ORNETTE COLEMAN

It is sobering to consider that when Mozart was my age he had already been dead for a year.

—TOM LEHRER

Generations, whatever their length, evolve in pairs, as obstreperous mother and pristine child. They breathe in binary form. Inhaled impression becomes exhaled expression, Victorians emerge into flappers, action into reaction. Sacred turns profane back to sacred, then profane once more and forever. New twists are added, unraveled, reinstated, again torn apart.

For instance, in movie females: the good lightness of Mae Marsh which once vanquished the bad blackness of Theda Bara was itself vanquished in the forties which introduced wicked blondes like the Lana Turner of *The Postman Always Rings Twice* or the Barbara Stanwyck (bewigged for the occasion) of *Double Indemnity* into contrast with the now-saccharine brunette of the Ann Rutherfords or Phyllis Thaxters. Dark Gail Patrick was no longer the "other woman." Then Marilyn brought back the Blonde as Victim, despite two wicked roles (*Niagara* and *Don't Bother to Knock*). As a sex, wicked or not, women are Out when men are In in the movies—as during war, which overlaps with peace, which overlaps. . . . Such men in their turn are pretty Valentinos superseded by virile Gables, superseded by pretty Powers, by virile Brandos, by pretty Dean, virile Belmondo, pretty Delon, ebb, flow and ebb. . . .

By the same token the sending of children to public rather than private schools, like circumcision practice (at least among upper-class American gentiles), alternates generations.

Similarly with music. Given eras stress length or height: counterpoint as opposed to harmony, vertical versus horizontal. The sophisticated linear represents, if you will, the "sacredness" of Palestrina, Bach, Reger, Schoenberg, Boulez; while the vulgar up-and-downness of the chordal signifies the "profanity" of Monteverdi, Beethoven, Chopin, Poulenc, Copland—who each settle neatly between the other five. We have just entered another harmonic period in both so-called Jazz and Classical, a relief for all audiences (of both classical and jazz) from the contrapuntal stress of the fifties and forties, which were releasing themselves from the harmonic prominence of the thirties and twenties, that were revolting against the teens, that were. . . .

As for *performing* musical personalities, they are just that—personalities—according to the sexual emphases of a particular epoch. Sexiness, and its projection, is individual. (Groups aren't sexy.) Collective singing, from Gregorian chant to rock-and-roll, tends to generalities, political or religious, both in spirit and text. By definition, during the decade after the war, the non-vocal contrapuntalists (in all musical expressions) were non-sexual, that being a "social" age; while individuals (read personalities) like Peggy Lee, Ruth Etting, Sinatra, were sexy *because* individual. Even Caruso or Tebaldi presented sexiness, take it or leave it.

If today is sexual, it's not sexy, being polymorphous; our trend is massive: the gang bang. The Beatles aren't sexy, and neither are the Doors despite promotional attempts to individualize one of them. Rock gangs just aren't preoccupied with sexiness any more than Nikolais' dance group canceling itself into a delicious blur. Even the powerful Paris personality of Jacques Brel, who composes both lyrics and music of the songs he performs alone, is in New York today promoted by an undifferentiatedly unprepossessing quartet.

That was written yesterday. Such generalities are idle maybe, but diverting, and do suggest. . . .

No, it's the first day of Spring, 1968, and the Beatles start to bore me. I just don't care now when *Time* relates a hullabaloo about their new trend, the reversion back to the straight rock of Presley. I seldom listen to them any more, yet still play *Socrate* once a week as I have for twenty years.

The shock in growing up—that everyone wasn't like me! I'd assumed the world was made of Hawthorne readers, Ravel listeners, Duchamp lookers, or of little boys who cut gym class to write music.

•

One indication that a thing may be good or "real" is that we become acquisitive, pre-emptive: we don't like people we don't like to like it, we want it for ourselves (and maybe certain friends) alone. This applies to literature somewhat, but mostly to music of "both sorts." It was true of the taste for Dostoevsky, Artie Shaw and Prokofiev in the thirties; for Kierkegaard, Billie Holiday and Berg in the forties; for Genet, Gerry Mulligan and Ives in the fifties; McLuhan, Joan Baez and Wolpe today. It defines In, Out having been let loose to the masses. When he whom we disdain loves our loves, those loves fall Out.

•

The point is relevant, though the examples may not be.

To criticize an example is irrelevant, since it belittles taste rather than challenging conception. To say that so-and-so's example of a said point is o.k. but incomplete, shows only what *we* would have given as example of that point, not the flaw in the point itself.

•

26 *August 1967*

The New York Review of Books now wants a piece on the Beatles. Amusing, suddenly, to be taken as a "serious" writer, to hoodwink the public as Picasso is still accused of doing! Now, if those accusers take *me* seriously, anything can happen: if *I* can be an authority in fancy mags (and what do I know? what can I learn from myself?), what hope then is there for the world? Like Lady Bird Johnson attending my music—has she nothing more important to do?

Being taken seriously as a composer is, however, I suppose, by now well entrenched (meaning that I also take it seriously), mostly because I get paid. Though to be taken seriously means to be grown up, and to be grown up is hard to swallow. (Notwithstanding Cocteau, who says childhood's what children seek to escape.) Students writing Doctor's dissertations on me "know" more about all music—including mine—than I do, yet they ask my advice. They ask it because they've seen my name in the paper. (Modesty forbids suggesting they may admire the music.) I smile inside. Yet I give the advice, and am right, righter than they; for the very idea of a Doctor's dissertation is wrong. Wrong, at least in this case, because necessarily incomplete where completion is all, and hence misrepresentative.

•

November 1967

Chappaqua's hero is no more distinguished than Auntie Mame, with whom he shares the same basic fault (though more pretentiously: in aiming higher he falls lower). Why should we be invited to *care* about Conrad Rooks any more than about Patrick Dennis' eccentric (by safe bourgeois standards) aunt?

Why, though, you ask, should we, in that case, care about Madame Bovary? Because Emma was Everywoman given the scalpel by an artist. Rooks is not Everyman, nor even Every-addict, but a special addict whose singularity lies not in artistry but in wealth. Mame is not Everywoman, nor even Every-kooky-aunt, but a special kooky aunt whose singularity lies not in goldheartedness but in wealth. Wealth then, not art or even interest, allows Mame and Rooks to single themselves out, to indulge their idiosyncrasies before an audience. Emma didn't single herself out, and the audience was Flaubert's.

●

My chief assessment of an individual is through his vulnerability. Finally I am drawn to him because of his susceptibility to hurt, his lack of self confidence. Genius aside, this seems always present in good artists, in attractive people. Which is precisely what made Monroe superior to Jayne Mansfield, made Johnson less appealing than Adlai Stevenson. It renders Lou Harrison more *attachant* than. . .

●

The playful fallibility of Bernstein! Though certainly as "famous" (if such things are judged) as, say, Albee, he appears to have more fun at it—the cold *power* of glory not being a concern.

●

Musical differentiations now should be Commercial and Non-commercial. Bernstein is both separately, Weill both at once, while Cage *seems* both, though in fact is neither. Non-commercial and commercial have always been distinctions one could draw from reference to individuals: Bach's cantatas vs. his piano fugues, Mozart's operas and quartets. We're told that Copland has two styles, hence two publics, one for the diatonic open spaces of *Rodeo*, another for the chromatic "urbanity" of *Connotations*. Vernon Duke—Vladimir Dukelsky—even uses two names for his two presumable audiences. But such audiences now are one. Nor have such distinctions ever been felt by Insiders.

•

More sound-alikes, each derived from "Goodbye Old Paint": Delius' *On Hearing the First Cuckoo*, Francaix' Piano Concertino (last movement), Rorem's *Design*, Copland's *Billy the Kid*.

•

If we steal we're also stolen from. What's new? The sun? Who's to judge? The good grasp what *is*, then shape it. *Myra Breckenridge* has rewritten my *Paris Diary*, no more, no less. And when I confided my two plays, *The Pastry Shop* and *The Young among Themselves*, to the author of *America Hurrah!* they turned up, device for device, in the final act of his trilogy. For musicians no less than for *littérateurs* (oh flagrant Shakespeare!) plagiarism is a prime prerogative.

•

My *Sun* is new, and so is television. At least they're new to me. But while my sun was robbed from a Pharoah and Byron and will continue shining, television dies forever every day. So television cannot be art, in our understanding of art as lasting— lasting like movies. Nor can television be a *medium* for art, either in itself or in retrospect (the late show), being by definition actual, reportage. Immediacy is television's power, and immediacy (the Seymour Krims notwithstanding) is but a lesser ingredient of art. *Amahl* is far better on stage than on camera. To pretend that TV can be meditative is as fallacious as the recording companies' justification of stereophonic sound, a sound that keeps composers awake and raging all night long.

•

Artists and their nocturnal emission, the agonizing midnight brainstorm that keeps them awake and constantly turning the light back on so as to notate notions in notebooks by the bed, mind on fire and far from sleep, prey to the ugly necessity of inspiration.

•

But the pang of no inspiration! How do we change? Need we? Each new work is undertaken not from experience but from scratch. The last work, like the last love affair, teaches us only what not to practice in the next; too late we learn that precisely the new avoidance of what then went wrong makes things go wronger now.

After becoming someone through work comes the problem of remaining someone, not through work but through the special responsibility of self-promotion, dear or cheap. Which precludes the work that made someone someone. The someone he remains is not the someone who first worked to become. So he now has become two ones, not working always, but playing at cats-cradle or at tossing a coin. No one knows him ever, nor even himself any more.

Where from here do I go, confronted by a clean sheet of empty staves? What notes inscribe? To state I will not follow electric paths rather than lead down my own pungent ones does not, for all its high individual intent, render me a leader, or even foster ideas.

To reread the old diaries does show I've changed. Today I couldn't be less interested in hanging out—taking the *time* to hang out—with the Great. Yet the change that not hanging out implies, doesn't fill those staves. So the musical change necessarily provoked by isolation has brought so far just a blank sheet to my lap. For refusal to jump on the safe bandwagon leaves nothing, nothing unsafe, to fall back upon, beyond the dubious praises of rarely inspired laymen.

•

Inspired laymen tell me that composers today are solving personal, not musical problems, by working toward, not within an expression. Young musicians, with their overdose of choice, don't know which way to compose. My laymen then lose interest, on discovering the composer isn't writing for them, or even for himself, but in order to solve an essentially non-musical question—intimate and/or mathematical.

Critics, too, today write around rather than about music. But they do write about themselves. The same holds for me. Yet when I reread those first notes-without-music as depicted in that ponderously derivative essay on Morocco which Cecil Smith requested for his *Musical America* back in 1949, I feel the present volume to be a bit more farsighted. Perhaps it's delusion, the fact being, as all my friends know, I've worn glasses for myopia since age thirteen. But better to be shot for an eagle than a mockingbird.

EZRA POUND AS MUSICIAN

•

At thirteen I knew backward Stravinsky's recording of Les Noces: *it was about grown-ups getting married. Last week I saw the Robbins ballet on this music: it was about two kids getting married. With a sigh I felt my age.*

—NED ROREM

NOTHING IS MORE BEMUSING THAN TO DISCOVER in reappraisal that certain opinions once voiced by the Truly Great now appear quite naïve. The discovery is bemusing (rather than exasperating) because it invariably occurs in areas outside the Great Man's "specialty." (Had he been naïve *within* that specialty he would not, by definition, have been great.)

Specialists are what artists (also scientists and candlestick makers) of our century mostly become*; if they develop an affection for one of the sister arts they fall prey to the same failings as any amateur: the confounding of acquaintance with knowledge, of conviction with greatness, effort with ability. One thinks of Claudel's or Henry James' verbalizations on painting—or this very remark on James and Claudel! When the concern is

---

* Or what they *became* during our first half-century. Today artists all are G.P.'s again—general practitioners. *C'est la grande pause.*

music, which it is here, a practicing musician merely smiles patiently as, say, André Gide tells him what Chopin is all about, or as E.M. Forster—even Shaw—explains the art through poetic rather than analytic description. Composers, of course, class performers as laymen, and consider men like Rubinstein or Casadesus as more sensical when playing than when writing, or writing about, music. Perhaps in a pinch a philosopher such as Susanne Langer can be attended precisely because she exorcises the phony inspirational Hollywoodiana from musical art.

Some poets are original and instructive when they discuss peripheral (i.e. theatrical) usages of music, sometimes even when they make librettos for their composer friends. But when venturing suggestions as to how their verse should be musicalized or how the music itself should be built, they tread risky water— the very water in which Ezra Pound nearly drowned.

Nearly, but not quite. Between the two is continuing life. And life, with all that implies of curiosity and scholarly enthusiasm, is what, in the 1920's, the poet had in abundance.

•

Music reportage is more appropriate for performance than for composition, for how the execution occurred than for what was executed, for what McLuhan calls (I think) the "hot medium" than for what stays put. Berenson wrote real literature about paintings of the past because those paintings are stationary (hence, paradoxically, continual): they can be *referred to*. But Shaw's criticism of 19th-century musical execution becomes (since the performance is gone forever) less literature than history. There exists today a whole new style of recording criticism, and records, like pictures, stay put. But since God didn't intend music to be heard on disks, such art is makeshift. (Occasional music *is* designed to be heard only on recording, although nothing could be more self-contradictory than, for example, a record of Chance Music—and several exist.)

As to the instructive virtue of musical criticism, it tells the public who wasn't there what happened last night, or the public who was there what to think about what happened last night. To composers it will teach nothing about the quality or construction of pieces (score-reading teaches that), but will maybe teach them something about how pieces can be played—including their own.

The Music Commentator, then, falls roughly into either of two classifications: 1) that of reporter on what just happened (press reviewer of concerts) or on what is happening (taste maker); 2) that of reporter on what once happened (historian, biographer) or on what was happening (authors on the evolution of harmony out of plain-chant and counterpoint).

Pound, by his own self-ordainment, becomes classified under each of these categories, though by what authority it is hard to say, for no one seems to know much about his formal musical training. He has, I'm told, passed much of his adult life in near contact with the once-successful violinist Olga Rudge; and during the twenties in France he hobnobbed (as did all literati) with various creative musicians, mostly American. One still suspects that his auditory education was come by less through discussion with these persons than through rigorous study of the prosodic values of Provençal, a language, like all others before the fifteenth century, quite intertwined with music. Certainly Pound's intellectual knowledge about music far surpassed his practical knowledge; his main concern (at least before meeting Antheil) seems to have been between words, word rhythms and music. "Poetry atrophies when it gets too far from music, music when it gets too far from the dance" (*ABC Of Learning*). Certainly emotional references to music are everywhere apparent in his verse, from *A Lume Spento* of 1908 to his 1956 translation of Sophocles' *Women of Trachis*. And names of musicians are scattered throughout the *Cantos*.

On this let me cite the triple-threat musician, my friend

Robert Hughes, who, in 1958, visited Pound at St. Elizabeth's and wrote me later as follows:

> I went down from Buffalo as part of a recorder quartet led by Forrest Read, a Pound scholar who has published on the Cantos (Columbia Univ. Press, if I remember correctly). We played Gabrieli *canzoni* out on the lawn for Pound and his wife, and Pound said it was only the second time he had heard live music during his incarceration there—the first time having been a pianist brought by Stokowski. In addition to the soprano recorder I had my bassoon along, and having read that Pound at one time had played the instrument I offered it to him. He declined saying that he gave it up in the 20's in order to take up boxing with Hemingway. I asked him about *Le Testament* and he said that as a consequence of the war he had no idea where the manuscript or a copy could be found. He did, however, say that he had a page or two of his unfinished opera *Cavalcanti* and promptly fetched it from his room. It looked like a Ruggles manuscript—very large notes scribbled on broad wrapping paper. We played it for him: a simple troubadour-type tune, not terribly distinguished as a melody, but with a certain grace and ease for the voice.

Le Testament? A lost manuscript? An unfinished opera?

Indeed yes! From his special knowledge Pound had, in the twenties, composed an opera. Whatever that opera's ultimate worth, is there another poet of the past two centuries who can claim as much?*

The text was drawn from Villon's *Grand Testament* (1461), a number of funereal bequests in whimsically argotic yet highly poignant medieval forms of versification. The resulting libretto (or should it be termed rather a *chant-fable?*) amounts to an intoned "autobiography" of François Villon, in one forty-minute act. The musical score itself is certainly the work of a non-profes-

---

* Wagner was not a poet who composed, but a composer who poeted, as was the late Marc Blitzstein, or Menotti and Gunther Schuller today.

sional, e.g., much more finicky for the eye than it need be for translation by the ear. Although George Antheil helped both in the exegesis and in the actual notation, the result remains that of an amateur: measures shifting from an unreasonably complex 5/8 to 13/16 to etcetera could easily be simplified and still provide the smooth modal vocality intended by the poet. Nevertheless a self-justifying foreword to the manuscript deserves quotation:

> This opera is made out of an entirely new musical technic, a technic, for certain, made of sheer music which upholds its line through inevitable rhythmic locks and new grips . . . a technic heretofore unknown, owing to the stupidity of the formal musical architects still busy with organizing square bricks in wornout . . . patterns . . . a powerful technic that grips musical phrases like the mouths of great poets grip words.
>
> There is really nothing more to say. Those *who want to understand*, will understand Villon.
>
> As the opera is written in such a manner so that nothing at all is left to the singer, the editor would be obliged if the singer would not let the least bit of temperament affect in the least the correct singing of this opera, which is written as it sounds! Please do not embarrass us by suddenly developing intelligence.

Paris thus heard it in 1926, and Virgil Thomson, who was there, declared "the music was not quite a musician's music, though it may well be the finest poet's music since Thomas Campion . . . and its sound has remained in my memory." The foreword's insecure insolence notwithstanding, the opera is of genuine and hauntingly unclassifiable beauty.

The beauty, though, was of such impractical difficulty, that it was not until 1962 that the opera received a second hearing in a version made for the BBC by the Canadian composer Murray Schafer. Such is the material of the music that, like the music of Moussorgsky which also is submitted to much rearrangement (or, more properly, like the *Art Of The Fugue*), *Testament* "speaks" as well in various instrumentations. The Paris version was apparently for only two human voices, solo violin (Olga Rudge) and *corne*, a twelve-foot instrument from medieval France. Schafer's bilingual rendition is much more sophisticated, using full chorus, several soloists, and a complex of instruments including saxophone, mandolin, and rattled bones.

A few summers ago Gian Carlo Menotti induced the poet from his Rapallo seclusion briefly to attend another performance (only the third—and the first one ever staged) of *Testament* at the Spoleto festival. In preparation for this event Menotti engaged two protégés, the bright composers Lee Hoiby and Stanley Hollingsworth, to revamp the work by shortening it and standardizing the notation. The result was then choreographed by John Butler and offered to an elite international public whose reception apparently included high respect, puzzled indignation, and a standing ovation. The ovation was as much for Pound-the-poet as for Pound-the-composer. As for Pound-the-man, his reaction to the spectacle is said to have been non-committal, even dazed, and his spoken preamble was preceded by an untheatrically long silence.

Silence has come to be the tone of Ezra Pound today. I for one, as a composer thinking of a poet, find the fact unutterably touching and telling—the silence in music, and from poetry, of one who once spoke perhaps not wisely but too well.

Robert Hughes said Pound thinks little now about his music of the past, that it is remote, like all our pasts, like dreams, and that he is, silently, completing his life of Cantos.

This then—a career as composer of a single opera performed but thrice over a forty-year interval—represents Pound's qualification as Music Commentator. A qualification *after the fact*— for his book, which is the object of this discussion, was begun as early as 1918 and published a year before the first presentation of the opera.

•

The title is *Antheil and the Treatise on Harmony with Supplementary Notes by Ezra Pound*. It is divided into four sections of unequal length: *The Treatise on Harmony, Antheil, William Atheling,* and *Varia*.

The style, unlike the author's music, is pontifical, tries for wit, sometimes achieves rapidity and wisdom, more often ponderousness. A cultured and imaginative lay-genius like Pound can insist on learning the hard way (i.e., on his own) what a trained professional was quite simply taught at school and takes for granted. The lay-genius will present the professional with his "unique" discoveries; but the professional, dull though he be, heaves a plaintive sigh for the genius, for the genius could have saved so much time by merely opening a book.

Pound gives us emotional talk on practical subjects, practical talk on esthetics. One quickly senses that, at least below the surface, he may feel less on home ground here as he speaks (so to speak) from outside in, than in, for instance, the *ABC of Reading*, his other scholarly treatise, where he really speaks from inside out. Though treatise this present work is not—which is precisely what saves it; it contains none of the documentary orderliness of the usual doctorate. The effect rather is one of obsessions fragmented into a manner both folksy and grand, occasionally incomprehensible, not unlike the utterances of Ives or even, curiously, John Cage's diary.

Antheil, who provides the impetus for the major portion of the volume, appears (despite Pound's obstinate veneration of him) to provide an excuse onto which the writer latches his theories—or rather his conclusions. By far the chief reason, in the cold of our time, to allow the hot air of these conclusions to flow interestingly over us, is the Man, now almost historical and certainly mute, who once so feverishly committed them to paper.

•

Part One, *The Treatise on Harmony*, starts right off with an unfair question (though who expects poets to be fair?):

"What, mon élève, is the element grossly omitted from all treatises on Harmony. . ."

Does the *élève* now stare blankly because he must assume there's just one reply to this broadly arbitrary, even gratuitous, query (a reply, what's more, unavailably cached somewhere within the questioner's smugness)? Supposing, however, the pupil answered: "The element of Space." Meaning that the psychic sense of a stationary (vertical) harmony, or any sequence of harmonies, shifts according to place, as when sounded in a deserted cathedral rather than a crowded chamber.

He would simply be wrong. For teacher's answer is: "The element of Time. The question of the time-interval that must elapse between one sound and another if the two sounds are to produce a pleasing consonance or an *interesting* relation, has been avoided."

Pleasing and *interesting* aside, this concept may be less unique than Pound realized, although in 1923 it was stimulating. To his credit he develops (or rather, randomly restates) this notion not with conclusions of eyes, which are only means in music, but always of ears, which are ends. His reactions were dictates of blood circulation, though not the blood of corpses. "Pure theory" (he cites Richter) cannot . . . concern itself with practice." And more deliciously (quoting one Sauzay): "Il faut se borner à penser que J.-S. Bach écrivait la musique par certains procédés dont la loi génerale nous échappe."

His concern with acoustics was as deeply special as that of, say, Lou Harrison today, yet always (and this is not so frequent as you'd think) as applied to *sound*, the audible glowing of nature as opposed to the "academicism [which] is not excess of knowledge [but] the possession of *idées fixes* as to how one should make use of one's data." Yet in his joy at debunking pedantry he could become inadvertently pedantic himself

("There is nothing sacred about the duration of the second," etc.), but his ultimate and whimsical wish was to render the physics of sound so complex that composers would grow discouraged, would "give up trying to compose by half-remembered rules, and really listen to sound." How even more welcome today, in the dreary ice of our "serious" musical fray, would be that warm wish come true!

One wonders how the impact of this opening chapter might have resounded were its spontaneous information better co-ordinated. Then again, co-ordination might have detracted from the rugged urgency which finally reaches us more as poetry than as knowledge—poetry, as everyone knows, dealing more with word-sequence than with idea.

•

George Antheil. His name to our young is not even a name, and his performances number zero. But yesterday he was not only the self-proclaimed *Bad Boy of Music*—such was titled his autobiography—but the official bad boy (or "leftist," as the avant-garde was then named) of most expatriate Twenties intellectuals, the literary ones rather more than the musical. Gertrude Stein received him, although she knew nothing of music; Virgil Thomson promoted him both in journalism and in the organization of far-out concerts; James Joyce, a great Purcell fancier, discussed him as the prime mover of the now common machinery-in-art movement, and even considered collaborating with him on an opera; while Hemingway owed to his influential relations the publication of *In Our Time*.

Mr. Pound it was, though, who eventually, for better or worse, immortalized him in the present book. The aging poet's apotheosizing of this very young composer amounts in fact to a conglomeration of *bon mots* on art, *bon mots* so occasionally cogent, yet wild that they become impossible to summarize other than by illustration.

Stravinsky is quickly put down in favor of (or, at best, equated to) Antheil:

> Stravinsky arrived as a comfort, but one could not say definitely that his composition was new music; he was a relief from Debussy; but this might have been merely the heritage of Polish folk music manifest in the work of an instinctive genius. . . . Stravinsky's merit lies very largely in taking hard bits of rhythm, and noting them with care. Antheil continues this; and these two composers mark a definite break with the "atmospheric" school; they both write horizontal music. . . .

Why was Stravinsky a comfort? And how—though it makes little difference—was his composition not "new"? Certainly he was less a "relief" from (and doubtless he himself would admit it) than a *continuation* or outgrowth of Debussy. It is unclear how Polish music was reflected in this oh-so-Russian; as for his being horizontal, if one must equate music to the linear, Stravinsky at least in the Twenties, was most certainly vertical— that is, harmonic.

Later remarks on Stravinsky provide their own commentary:

> The "Sacre" stands, but its cubes, solid as they are, are in proportion to (Antheil's) Ballet Mécanique as the proportions of architecture are to those of town planning. . . . "Noces" falls to pieces. After the Ballet it sounds like a few scraps of Wagner, a Russian chorale (quite good), a few scraps of Chopin, a few high notes "pianolistic."

Good God! But then Pound is elsewhere correct in maintaining that the "authentic genius will be as touchy . . . about the differences between his own particular art and all others, as, or than, he will about any possible analogies with the arts."

> Antheil has . . . noted his rhythms with an exactitude, which we may as well call genius . . . has purged the piano, has made it into a respectable musical instrument. . . . Antheil is probably the first artist to use machines, I mean actual modern ma-

chines, without bathos." [There is nowhere mention of Varèse.] "I think that music is the art most fit to express the fine quality of machines. Machines are now a part of life. . . . A painting of a machine is like a painting of a painting. The lesson of machines is precision, valuable to the plastic artist, and to literati. . . .

Then he approvingly quotes Antheil: " 'the failure of Stravinsky(!). . . . In accepting Satie as a master, we see that he (Stravinsky) was nothing but a jolly Rossini.' "

This chapter elsewhere offers such tantalizing propositions as: "Prose is perhaps only half an art . . . you cannot get a word back into the non-human." Then it moralizes in a manner so *démodé* that the eyebrows of a Larry Rivers today, or even of a Boulez, would scarcely be raised; while a Frank O'Hara could only agree about longevity as it pertains to artists rather than to their work, artists seldom any more seeming to care about posterity, or even about the word Art: "The thorough artist is constantly trying to form an ideograph of 'the good' in his art; I mean the ideograph of admirable compound-of-qualities that make any art permanent."

Pound goes on to quote appraisals by Antheil himself, Antheil who notes a "constant tirade against improvisation": "Debussy, soul of ardent virgin, clear and sentimental implanted in great artistic nature." (Ironically, Debussy's own assessment of Grieg had not been too unlike this, and—if you will—equally "false": he compared the Norwegian's music to the sounds heard in Old Folks' Homes, to the taste of bonbons stuffed with snow!).

Antheil is finally defined by Pound as "possibly the first American or American-born musician to be taken seriously . . . (who) has made a beginning; that is, in writing music that couldn't have been written before."

Since any composer worthy of the name, be he "conservative" or "experimental," writes music that by definition couldn't have been written before, Antheil's fellow-musicians of this period were mostly a good deal more resistant to him than were the authors. He himself, a few years later, whether by abandon or ousting or nostalgia, quit the French musical scene for California, where he continued to turn out vast amounts of not-too-often-played scores (influenced no less by machines than by Hedy Lamarr, to whom his *Heroes of Today* is dedicated), and to write journalism on subjects quite unrelated to his field. In 1959 he died in comparative obscurity, and to date his music has not been revived, by either the Right or the Left.

What did Antheil think of Pound's overly personal, often disordered and irrelevant, yet highly sychophantic *précis* of his *oeuvre*? In the postwar retrospect of 1945 he tells us:

> It seems terribly unfair of me, at this time, to proceed to criticize Ezra Pound, now that the poet has fallen into disgrace. But, I emphasize, I would write these pages exactly this way if Ezra had become an international hero instead. For from the first day I met him Ezra was never to have even the slightest idea of what I was really after in music. I honestly don't think he wanted to have. I think he merely wanted to use me as a whip with which to lash out at all those who disagreed with him, particularly Anglo-Saxons; I would be all the more effective in this regard because I was an "unrecognized American."

And he beautifully adds: "The main clues of a composer's life are in his music; but it is not always so easy to read them."

And how do Antheil's surviving peers esteem him? Well, listen for instance to the 1967 assessment by Peter Yates who, in my opinion, is now America's leading spokesman for twentieth-century music:

> . . . the young American George Antheil [took] what then seemed the obvious course of using noise without exploring it. Antheil's explanations after the event tried to rationalize a successful headline-seeking stunt into a considered esthetic achievement. In fact, it was most successful in its headlines.

The sound lacks variety; the typewriters used for instruments do not compete effectively with the several pianos; the pianos are borrowed from Stravinsky's far more successful use of them in *The Wedding*; the airplane propeller is no more than Strauss's wind-machine in *Don Quixote*; and the rattling and banging of the percussive elements do not combine to produce musical substance. Similar faults are evident in much of the noise-music which has been composed since that time. Antheil's superficiality became more evident in later compositions, imitating the surfaces of more competent composers.

Or listen to the Britisher, Wilfrid Mellers, who (partly from the objectivity that springs from physical distance, partly from the subjectivity of a truly devoted love for us), in 1965, published the most definitive book to date on American music:

> . . . Antheil claims that [*Ballet mécanique*] is built mathematically on the Time-Space concept, like musical engineering, or modern architecture in sound. He admits that Varèse preceded him in this concept. In any case, compared with the works of Stravinsky and Varèse, *Ballet mécanique* has only historical, not musical interest. . . . [He] used arithmetical durations of silence as early as 1924, partly as a result of studying Oriental music. . . . [However], the work's motor rhythms relate it to Western music, and it does not get far with the space-time concept.

Or to the 1966 avowal of a personal sponsor from their mutual hey-day, Virgil Thomson, who presumably needs no introduction:

> My estimate [in 1926] of him as "the first composer of our generation" might have been justified had it not turned out eventually that for all his facility and ambition there was in him no power of growth. The "bad boy of music" . . . merely grew up to be a good boy. And the *Ballet mécanique*, written before he was twenty-five, remains his most original piece.

•

Like the pseudonymous Monsieur Croche behind whom Debussy hid, like Bernard Shaw's Cornetto di Basso, indeed like many a 19th-century critic who, for one or another reason (usually to protect professional status) adopted a false cognomen, Ezra Pound from 1917 to 1920 wrote fortnightly in the *New Age* under the pen name of William Atheling. In 1923 these admittedly ill-written musical "siftings" were submitted to Antheil who bestrewed them with marginalia. This conjointed enterprise constitutes the third, and probably most personal, portion of Pound's treatise. Most personal—partly because Antheil's italicized interpolations are fairly incidental agreements and none too witty (examples: "A bad musician will only admit a name so well-known that there can be no question about it. He is a bad musician because he has no 'guts' anyway"; or, commenting on a remark that the British concert-performer is chosen from the exclusively eviscerated strata of the community: "How funny it must be in England"; or: "I bow gracefully"; or simply: "Bravo!!"), and partly because here Pound expounds on what, instinctively, a great poetical layman can most "know" about: performance (as opposed to composition), and what he terms the "musicking" of verse, namely prosody.

A telling wisdom careens in the wake of platitude: "Hundreds of musical careers have been muddled because performers have not understood how entirely music must lead its own life; must have its own separate existence apart from the audience. . . ." Then: "An era of bad taste probably gathers to itself inferior matter from preceding periods. An indiscriminate rummaging in the past does not help to form a tradition."

Still, when talking of Words & Music, he deserves quotation in any (but there *aren't* any!—except my own, and I didn't know Pound then) manual on How to Make a Song:

> There are different techniques in poetry; men write to be read, or spoken, or declaimed, or rhapsodised; and quite differently to be sung. Words written in the first manners are

spoiled by added music; it is superfluous; it swells out their unity into confusion. When skilled men write for music then music can both render their movement . . . tone by tone, and quantity by quantity; or the musician may apparently change the word-movement with a change that it were better to call a realisation. Music is not speech. Arts attract us because they are different from reality. Emotions shown in actual speech poured out in emotion will not all go into verse. The printed page does not transmit them, nor will musical notation record them phonographically.

Thematic invention in music has coincided with periods when musicians were intent on poetry, intent on the form and movement of words. Thematic invention is the weakest spot in contemporary music *everywhere*. The rhythms of French are less marked, but only in France do we find a careful study of the verbal qualities. I do not think I have shown any delirious or unbalanced appreciation of the modern French, but among their song-setters are practically the only contemporary song-setters whom one can respect.

The best poets have been nature poets only incidentally. Nature appears here and there in their work, but is not singled out for their subject-matter. Whatever "religion and Christianity" may still mean to the populace and to the modern heath-dweller, religion as exploited by artists of the last century has been mostly exploited as convenient furniture and not from any inner necessity.

One might take exception to other of his song-writing generalities:

The perfect song occurs when the poetic rhythm is in itself interesting, and when the musician augments, illumines it, without breaking away from, or at least without going too far from the dominant cadences and accents of the words; when ligatures illustrate the verbal qualities, and the little descants and prolongations fall in with the main movements of the poem.

Still we will all agree that

> In the finest lyrics the music so comes from the words and enriches, reinforces, illuminates them. We will recapture this art of illuminating only when we have musicians capable of literary discrimination, capable of selecting *cantabile* words, and of feeling the fine shades of their timbre, of their minor hurries and delays.

Other jewels can also be detached from their setting and thrown out loose here:

> Our decadence may be due to the fact that the educated are now too stupid to participate in the arts.
> You cannot compare Music since Beethoven with the early thin music which is like delicate patterns on glass. Since Beethoven people have thought of music as of something with a new bulk and volume.
> One must, perhaps, find one's ideal artists in fragments, never whole and united.
> Tchaikowsky: a certain cheapness is imminent in this composer. He is not cheap all the time, or even, perhaps, most of the time but he keeps one in a state of anxiety.

Occasionally there is a *gaffe* like "we noticed how STUPID Liszt was, and how little he knew about chords" (if Liszt didn't know about chords, nobody did!), followed by facile banality like "opera is a diffuse form . . . made to cover light afterdinner conversation," followed by pedantic advice like "it is a good thing for singers to get off the beaten track and hunt up music that is lying in desuetude." (Most music lying in desuetude lies there because God—meaning Lack of Talent—willed it so.)

Special divisions in a similarly inconsistent genre are devoted to the piano (called pye-ano), to the fiddle, to the *lieder* school ("which is wrong"), to ballet, to Chopin and Scriabin and Mozart; and deep in the morass shines a gemlike essay on oriental music as compared to Provençal poetry.

The whole comes off as a succinct cluster of aphoristic Gallic *pensées* translated into the grouchiest Americanese.

•

Varia gives us more of the same, though chiefly directed toward composers. The bulk originally appeared in the *New Masses* and in *The New Criterion*.

Composers are all too aware of being at "the mercy of the executant, [who] is at the mercy of his endocrines," but they may be amused to see their craft reduced to "knowing what note you want; how long you want it held; and how long one is to wait for the next note, and in making the correct signs for these durations." Pound smartly adds that "it is for lack of just such simple statements . . . that the misunderstandings arise between the musician and the well wisher"; then, for the first time in the whole book, qualifies his authority: ". . . apart from accommodating notes to words, I am an incompetent amateur."

This very amateurism led this very professional Idaho poet, while he was overwhelming world scholarship, to wish to do as much for musical art. That wish was therefore to prove that George Antheil had taken, "or at any rate (had) found a means that can take, music out of the concert hall." This removal presumably would disseminate formal sound throughout an even vaster world than his own literary one, and bestow it upon the people as tribal ceremonies had been bestowed in the past, or sea chanties or labor songs. Such has ultimately occurred moreover, for better or worse, through our John Cage, who would be pleased to read that the "aesthete goes to a factory . . . and hears *noise*, and goes away horrified; . . . the composer hears noise, but he tries to (?) 'see' (no, no), he tries to *hear* what kind of noise it is." Indeed, Antheil *had* talked vaguely of "tuning up" whole cities, of "silences twenty minutes long *in the form*" etc., though never put these functions to the test.

Antheil, by our witness today and by his admission yesterday, served as sacrificial goat for a genius whose *gauche prévoyance* had, in itself, little influence, but was in fact an image of what, distortedly, would come to pass. If for no other reason then, Pound's treatise is worth a re-perusal. For strange as it may seem, few scholars know of this book, though they've hazily heard of Pound's opera, while few musicians know of the opera though they've hazily heard of this book.

Any jottings of the Great (Pound was and is great), even a *billet-doux* or laundry list (and this volume is much more than that), become, by definition, important, deserving the concentration of cultured laymen and all other fellow-artists.

ELEVENTH INTERLUDE

A few weeks before his death in 1963 Jean Cocteau composed
this drawing as a cover for my setting of Elizabeth Bishop's
Visits to St. Elizabeth's. That long and snowballing poem—a sort
of macabre "House That Jack Built"—describes Miss Bishop's
seeing Ezra Pound at the hospital in 1957. The drawing seems
appropriate here between these chapters, since I knew and
admired Cocteau (he provided me with several such musical
covers), who knew and admired Pound (Pound used Jean's
name as sole timely reference in the opera *Testament*), who
was an admiration of Elizabeth Bishop (her first name is spelled
in the drawing *à la française*), who is an admiration of mine
(I, who have never seen Ezra Pound).

I'D TAKE THE FIRE

•

"Je sens une difficulté d'être." *Thus did Fonte-*
nelle, the centenarian, reply when he was dying
and his doctor asked: "M. Fontenelle, what do you
feel?" Only his belonged to his last hour. Mine has
been from the beginning.

—JEAN COCTEAU

ONE RAINY AFTERNOON IN 1951 DURING MY
first visit to the meridional chateau of the remarkable Vicomtesse
de Noailles (she who had commissioned *The Blood of a Poet*),
I found on her shelves a ragged first-edition of Cocteau's *La
Difficulté d'être*. Beneath its disturbing title the author had auto-
graphed a medieval sleeve from which emerged gaunt fingers
clutching a plume, bewitched and still moving in that famous
starry scrawl: *Chère amie, comment vous dédicacer un tel livre!*
The charitable implication that she too shared his seeming ease
for such beauty as distinguishes an artist from his fellow man
is perhaps what led the Vicomtesse lately to declare of her childhood: "I was Jean's Lolita."

We all felt that, even before we knew him. Authors we love
we "relate" to, we think we'd get on with them, yearn for their
living contact. Jean Cocteau's literary humanity provoked this

yearning more than any artist of our time. As unsolved crimes are often confessed to by innocent old ladies, or as New York bars still harbor septuagenarians who swear they are "layers" of Djuna Barnes' model for Doctor O'Connor, so the city of Paris once swarmed with siblings claiming to be the original *enfants terribles* from whom their fabulous friend had fired a masterpiece. Such claims are usually unproductive and always fallacious: "People do not read but read themselves." After the fact and by association the models base themselves on the masterpiece, forgetting that a writer is only a writer when he's writing —that "awake," he's as ordinary as anyone.

Except Cocteau! He early learned from his junior Radiguet that an artist by definition cannot be ordinary, that he has only therefore to write like others to appear extraordinary. And the extraordinary oozed like ectoplasm into his waking hours too; to meet him—however briefly—was indeed to know him, to be momentarily endowed with his *ease of beauty*.

The ease of beauty. But at what a price—ease is so hard! All in the end is resolved except the enigma of existence ("It must be a dream that one can live at ease in one's own skin"), though from the poet's bloody plume the attempted resolution itself shapes art, art with its urgent imperfections, for beauty limps.

•

I mulled the yellowing leaves of this book until the rain had cleared into an April sunset, by which time I sensed a new contact with the *flesh* of the man (for the man in person was contradictorily a skeleton of his product), recalling how I too had first come to know him, to *want* to know him. In Chicago, aged thirteen, David Sachs, not without malice, lent me those novels which were to pervade my thinking as insidiously as Huysmans' pervaded that of Dorian Gray. The next few years produced for those of our milieu the gospel of Cocteau's first three movies. And he knew then what now we've come to know:

that films, not the stage, are such stuff as dreams will all be made on. His dream of "Beauty and the Beast" he brought to America himself in 1948 when we all went to examine him at a Gotham Book Mart cocktail. (He arrived very late. Where had he been? In Harlem, it seems, to find an inpecunious old friend, the former world champion Al Brown). With Paul Goodman as makeshift translator (we knew French then, but not how to talk it) we applauded the verbal acrobatics of our current world champion who then bowed himself out of the shop and into the night of his new Manhattan, which suddenly we too found rich and strange. He led us to our own water—a fountain of youth—and showed us how to drink.

I cannot know whether his Catholic way of drinking, rather than the Quaker romanticism of my infancy, turned me into a Frenchman rather than a German (we are all culturally one or the other), but it did lead me to Paris which became a second home where I would risk the dangers of disillusion by encountering unsuspected aspects of a legend. Only presumption could claim my reportage now as singular, as more qualified than another's, as "truth"—though at least my truth is my own and I long to share it. That's just the point: Cocteau's very nature (nature or magic?) impels preemption in his fans.

Thus it was that six months previous to the wet April day of which I speak—on October 6, 1950, to be precise—I first visited the skeleton in the flesh.

•

"You yourself must find a way to meet me—miracles work better than appointments," was his challenge to my letter. Human intercourse was for him a game, but the rules were easily learned. I "found a way" and we made a date. Then I panicked. You don't *meet* idols, they don't exist on mortal terms. Jean-the-Artist had spellbound three European generations: Diaghilev's demand, "Astound me," unleashed in 1912 a talent which, until the last war's end, had dazzled every class with its ballets and monologues, movies and plays, its novels and essays, poems and paintings, even its choreography (if as a musician Cocteau lacked a voice, he compensated by "inventing" Satie and the *Groupe des Six*). Jean-the-Man had been no less formidable: had he not inherited from Wilde the title of "the world's most brilliant talker"? and from De Quincey that of the world's most conspicuous *opiomane*? Was he not haunted by the melancholy suicides of so many whose strength was unequal to his? Had not *Le Livre blanc* described his parties in Toulon brothels? Had he not attended operas with Barbette, the Texan trapezist in drag, and created and destroyed names now more legendary than his own? Had not Gide monumentalized him (if dubiously) as Passavant in *The Counterfeiters*, and Freud himself dissected his *Sang d'un Poète*? If to a continental admirer the image of Cocteau was awesome, how much more so was the fact to a young American weaned on the glamorous Eternal Return!

It was eleven o'clock of a perfect morning. He himself welcomed me into his small apartment overlooking those gray gardens harboring hordes of screeching children, long rows of chestnut trees, and the expensive Véfour restaurant. After telling the housekeeper not to disturb us until one, the *maître* followed me into a tiny red room and locked the door. The red room contained a tiny crimson bed heaped with recent art reviews (all had uncut pages), a telegraph set (out of order), a ceiling-high blackboard displaying a boy's scarlet chalk profile, a Siamese cat (female), and a pervading heady fragrance (opium maybe). Through his window echoed the real world, laughing games and fountains plashing, and across the courtyard I recognized the yellow blinds of Colette's casements. (But he has described it all in *On the Palais Royal*.)

Tall thin Cocteau seemed agitated, explained he'd come home only minutes before I rang, had been to check up on *le père Gide* from whom he'd gotten a *pneumatique* in a disquieting handwriting. I was impressed that he had nonetheless found time to don a floor-length azure robe. The long sleeves hid his hands, though in reinforcing each *bon mot* (three a minute) he pointed skyward and the famous fingers shot forth like antennae. Like antennae too were his great ears, his rebellious kinky hair, even his voice which listened while it spoke in a timbre unrelated to the one we knew from records—higher, less mundane, more insistent. Insistent it was as he incessantly moved, never sitting, a jittery jaguar forever pacing, occasionally petting the sister Siamese in passing, talking, talking in phrases that bristled with *con* and *emmerder* ripe as forbidden fruit to my would-be obstreperous but puritan taste. Yet this congested atmosphere seemed all elegance without the crumbling corners one finds in even the richest old French homes. For my host was young. Desperately.

At no time did I sense the lazy-hot mystery which proved so fatal to Maurice Sachs and others here in former decades. Nor did I find him beautiful. He did strike me as—well—more *engagé* than I'd have guessed, for France in those days swarmed with his tired replica. Now here was the real thing, and oh, what posture! What thin lips releasing from the true source such a thick sheen of verbs! My own talk was reticent, but since he ended all phrases with a brutal *quoi!* or *hein!* I couldn't not reply. My dull answers he shined up with his own tongue, then spit them like sparks back into my dazed features, while paradoxically putting me at ease—*including* me.

"We must know what we're doing, we poets, and know well, even if not why. Remain comrades. . . . They call me robber. But of course! They're right for the wrong reasons, *ces cons-là!* Poetry comes from elsewhere, an uninvited guest. Doesn't your music? That music, those poems themselves steal from *us*. . . . They call me liar. Aren't beautiful lies what all children know as fairy-tales? Certainly each child lies; but when he succeeds in revamping his lie as personal expression—why he becomes

immense, *quoi!* Do you not do the same? . . . Art's not on a
page, not in the concert hall, or at least not *only*. It's a snake,
a river, a vine twisting all over from high to low, shrinking in its
growth, expanding to become anyone's little perilous property.
Listen! say listen there, come to the window! Hear that *ouvrier*
down there? He's whistling the bassoon solo from the *Sacre*. It
belongs to *him* now!" [The tune in fact was *La Vie en Rose*,
which in any case would have proved his point.] "Kinsey interviewed you? Really? We French, you know, are more amused
than intrigued by your charts and lists, by your slow psycho-
analysis—*that* we've had, known, used, abandoned. We don't
specialize like you, but scatter our seed—*si j'ose dire*—to insemi-
nate all manner of fauna, *hein!* Yet he's right, your Kinsey, to
request genital data from his worried clients. Everything counts
in a man—*et je ne crois guère aux hommes de petite verge*. . . .
My voice, you say, sounds like whose? like Yves Salgues'? You
hear him through me but uttering different things and grow
confused? *Mon pauvre ami*. We too were confused, but poets:
making order in the form of disorder, aristocrats with the faces
of anarchists. But oh, today! You. . . ."

I had no reason to think that the same disk might not be put
on for the next tourist who came knocking (and what of it?).
I do remember that he gave of himself with more immediacy
than I've ever known. Yet he warns us in these pages that "to
receive all the callers in despair is impossible. . . . Let us beware
of the drowning who cling to us and who drown us." Perhaps
because precisely I was not drowning (not yet) I could grasp
his coherence of the unrelated, could comprehend what people
meant by his encounter and friendship being one. Like our
Frank O'Hara he gave himself promiscuously in speech, a lover
without contact—which is to say without ulterior motive. This
violent lack of motive is rare and hypnotic. Cocteau's sorcery was
in sympathy, a sympathy of perceptive monologuing which
caused even fools to feel a fair exchange. So he swayed millions,

wholesomely or injuriously, depending on who could keep that unalterable pace which he maintained went faster than beauty and converted the ordinary into works of art.

The "ordinary" that morning grew from talk of passion and crime in American towns into procedures of so-called creation and the creator's social location. His verb for the creative act was *chier* (*"Quand j'ai chié mon Orphée!"*). "Artists must stay put, grow ever more selfish, never seek to rearrange the world. They must—and from the start, like me—create and live by their own mythology, discovering for its expression the mystic force hidden within the rough state [*l'état brut*] of the medium itself—the bronze, the words, the notes, whatever—all these lead a life of their own and lead us with them, as mathematicians are led, are magnetized, by the more-than-human power of numbers. Artists *must* because they have no choice but to be exorcised only to be re-enslaved."

Cocteau's words, like nature, were an overflow, an *embarras de richesses* from which his work was ultimately tailored with the economy of a diamond-cutter. He was nevertheless not so uneconomical as to avoid looking at his watch. Suddenly my two hours were gone.

A warm *au revoir* sent me off through the children's garden, passing beneath Colette's window, to have lunch alone—not at the Véfour but in a bistro across the Seine. There I pondered the verb *to know well* which, after all, has little to do with longevity or habit, but with intensity and exchange. Because I was feeling —bouyantly, if gullibly—that on that autumn noon I had made a friend.

•

In September of 1963 he mailed me what may have been his final drawing, a sketch I'd requested to illustrate my setting of Elizabeth Bishop's *Visits to St. Elizabeth's*. His accompanying letter was signed: *"Avec la tendresse fidèle d'un pauvre malade*

dont la convalescence sera très lourde et très longue." Two weeks
later he died. Maybe that little fortnight was indeed *très longue*.
In any event I found his handwriting (and he always wrote by
hand, in a script as carnavalesque as his oratory) now as disquieting as he had found Gide's thirteen years earlier—and as
my own may be found sooner than I think.

During those thirteen years we engaged in regular correspondence, his side including always one of those drawings with
which he was so lavish, or a book of new poems "thrown to the
sea like a bottle containing my gentlest thoughts." And we were
to meet again a dozen times, at Hervé Dugardin's or Marie
Laure's, at the Aurics' or *chez les duchesses*, at backstage brawls
or noble picnics. For his life glared socially as it did industriously,
and everywhere he set the tone. Or hoped he did. The fact
was that after forty virtuosic years his prestige (not to mention
his productive vitality) was in decline, at least for youth, which
comprises that public most needed by aging geniuses. But youth's
needs were elsewhere. Not too slowly but all too surely French
fantaisistes and poets were being replaced by artistic philosophers
and practical proselytizers.

Cocteau's sleight-of-hand had for awhile dissembled a lack of
discrimination. More than anyone he combined the sublimely
right with the unutterably trashy. Who else could so wonderfully announce, "One must know how to go too far" (he later
credited this quip—though not publicly—to Péguy), and then
pervert himself in an official address to Marlene Dietrich,
"Madame, your name starts with a caress and ends in a whip-
lash!"? Who else could summon tears so purging (although
Stravinsky now finds them bathetic) as those implied at the end
of *Oedipus Rex*, "Farewell, we loved you," and the next day
accept a sum from a stocking manufacturer for the slogan:
"Ladies, your limbs are poems: bind them in our hose"? If in
the twenties he promoted such diverse talents as Braque and the
Fratellini Brothers, in the thirties Jean Marais and Edith Piaf,

and in the forties Jean Genet and Maurice Gendron, he endorsed with equal vim a series of mediocrities.

All this was valid, fun, fruitful, indeed quite like the non-specialist Frenchmen whose "inspired Jean" outdid them all as Renaissance Man. But with World War II and the advent of Existentialism his wand lost its power—he waved and no one looked. Enthusiasm alone couldn't hold the stage, and novelty changes meaning when years roll by, as a star changes meaning when telescopes approach. Cocteau's star—the signature that was his heart—dimmed drastically in 1953. He lay near death for weeks and was already mourned by *les vieux petits amis*. He had been struck by that same stone snowball that literally broke two of his hero's hearts—"the marble fist blow which brings beauty, quick to the heart, in passing." But he performed a new miracle by recovering. This time everyone looked as he secured for himself that most coveted of cultural thrones, a chair in the French Academy. Such an honor had been systematically denied all "unconventional" authors from Baudelaire to Sartre.

Being thus immortalized in life Cocteau, as though by agreement with the angel of his mythology, suffered another slump. Officially a great man, his last ten years produced little of apparent consequence beyond two excellent books of poems and one fair movie. He did make of his protégé a legal heir (at present under dispute), allow himself to be pictured cutting capers with Chaplin or Picasso, and appear at concerts to boo or cheer when booing and cheering no longer of themselves proved much. He did, also, contribute prefaces and blurbs (less influential now than Sartre's) and continue until the end in the practice of generous acquaintanceship. But his stylish rage and vigor were collapsing. Finally, the eleventh of October 1963, on learning of the premature death of his old friend Edith Piaf, he too died—from pure sympathy, one almost feels—at his country home in Milly, uttering the strangely bland (for him) epigram: "The ship is going down."

If a dying artist has the consolation that his works may live on, the terrible question arises: which ones? That Cocteau should quit this earth in hand with Piaf seemed to us then a final homage to the art of love; today, with the irony of perspective, it looks like a classical bit of upstaging. For the theater was Cocteau's most telling milieu, and whether or not he created directly for it, his whole output including his daily life was essentially dramatic. It seems unlikely, however, that his professional collaborations with the rare Edith in 1940 stand much chance of survival except as exercises in jargon. *Le Fantôme de Marseille*, about a woman whose sweetheart is murdered while masquerading *en travestie*, and particularly *Le Bel Indifférent*, about the same woman with a mute lover, now read like tryouts for the superb *Voix Humaine*, which remains a masterpiece both in its original black and white version, and in the ensuing heartbreaking technicolor of Poulenc. Basically theatrical are his nine movies from *Le Sang d'un Poète* to *Orphée*, and also of course his fifteen odd stage works from *Antigone* through *Bacchus*— not to mention lesser monologues for Berthe Bovy and Marianne Oswald, or ballets for Massine and Babilée. But theatrical too (by which I mean visual, kinetic—given to move, literally, the beholder) are his introspective verses from the very early *Vocabulaire* to his late *Claire-Obscure*, and even his criticism, from those first early "notes about music" (*Le Coq et l'Arlequin*) in 1918 to *La Démarche d'un Poète*, 1953.

And so, finally, are these "objective" essays (*La Difficulté d'être*) which, with their sequel, *Journal d'un Inconnu*, constitute a series one might term Dramatic Abstractions on such diversities as his own body, frivolity, youth, France, dreams, customs, or reading. But he was a poet, a painter, and a child as well, and blended the three.

Like all true poets he anticipates science when speaking here of, say, pain. (As to whether—as he maintains—he actually wrote of pain while in pain is as irrelevant as in his *Opium*. One does not, for example, write about mescalin while under it; you can't do two things at once: feel pain and objectify the feeling. What *is* relevant is that he makes *us* feel it.)

Like all true painters he confronts his witness with an animate object when dealing with, say, death. He shows what it is like *to wake up dead!* His continual obsession with mirrors taught us that they are the doors through which death comes and goes. ("Look at yourself all your life in the mirror and you'll see Death working like bees in a glass hive.")

Like all true children he finds good in evil when talking, say, of haunted houses, as he does in a piece called just that, or in his skit *La Farce du Château.* ("They imitate us and only offer us what we give them. But this echo speaks and insists on dialogue.")

His own haunted house was formed from transparent stained glass of the queerest hues, although his domesticity was never—except by allusion—a subject for his prose, as it was for the otherwise more circumspect Gide. Perhaps the present volume comes closer than others to revealing a bare heart, yet the revelations no sooner advance than they recede in waves of tantalizing generality. ("I dare not confess here, even though I am resolved to tell all . . ."; ". . . it is not just a defense mechanism against sickness which forces me to write this particular book.") Finally the waves freeze into essays as succinct as those of Bacon or Hazlitt, if more compassionate.

For compassionate he was, and, like any artist, utterly vulnerable, but vulnerable *with tact.* By all this I mean that personal sexuality (except in the pseudonymous *Livre blanc* or various unsigned illustrations for Genet) was never his professional theme, though God knows it was often a send-off—as with most intellectuals—for blooming conversation.

Conversation, until 1950, was an art and a pleasure, and Jean was France's chief professor of it. Surrounded, always surrounded he was, like Andy Warhol now, by leeches and aspirers and—who knows?—genius (though could Malanga be compared to Radiguet?); yet where Warhol is mute, Cocteau was eloquent. At the start he too surrounded (if one person can be said to surround) learning, learning with listening eye and watchful ear. As sensitive to the verb as his predecessor Anna de Noailles, and to nature as his neighbor Colette herself, he tells of conversations with microbes and the very thoughts of plants (see *On Laughter, On Beauty*). Where McLuhan today promotes a touching if clumsy faith in the artist as the only one "who knows," Cocteau yesterday, *being* an artist, spoke with truth that was more than truth of poets "who commit themselves for no other reason than to lose."

•

Yet three generations had stylishly misrepresented Cocteau as at worst a liar, at best a conjurer (how impatient he was with that word!). Perhaps I too have so misrepresented him in the foregoing. Yet he *was* a conjurer in that, as the serious thinker he has proven himself to be, he converted impossibly sluggish minds into poetic participants. And he *was* a liar in that, as he pointed out, his were "true lies," and he borrowed plots (as did Shakespeare) indiscriminately. Certainly his *Eternel Retour* or *Les Parents Terribles* are no closer in intention to Tristan or the so-called Boulevard Comedies than are, for instance, Albee's *Zoo Story* to *The Blue Hotel* of Stephen Crane, or James' *Roderick Hudson* to *La Peau de Chagrin* of Balzac.

But three generations also hailed Cocteau as a prophet. Are not his initials, after all, those of Jesus? and his trademark the Star of Bethlehem flashing like a flying saucer? And if that flash now sometimes illuminates the *démodé*, at its keenest it pierces like a laser beam straight into the human heart and moves it as no Gallic philosopher has moved it since. Cocteau's curiosity about all matters, at home and abroad and in the cosmos, was healthily untypical of his countrymen so drably self-confined within their frontiers.

This hearty motion, then, will possibly have been Cocteau's lasting contribution. And not, curiously (at least for me), as exemplified in the plays, but in the two strange novels, *Thomas l'Imposteur* and *Les Enfants Terribles*, wherein the author's recurring theme of fatality hits hardest.

Despite a tardy if vague awakening, France, with her blindness to outside energy and adherence to national tradition, has grown increasingly moribund in fancy. This has never seemed more true than today when so many of her principal spokesmen are left unreplaced in death. Cocteau had invented a France of his own, then invited others to wax and shimmer among his magic flames which colored every aspect of the land where now only an afterglow remains.

That country adores categoric generalities. A literary monthly once posed this familiar question to several writers: If your house were burning down and you could take away just one thing, what would it be? "I'd take the fire," answered Jean Cocteau. And he did.

Recalling Martha

No one can remember exactly what she says.
—AGNES DE MILLE

They are autoerotic and have no conversation.
—VIRGIL THOMSON

New York, Autumn 1945

She is to theater what Garbo is to dance. An actor within her medium, while Garbo dances on film.

Good dancers are rarer than good pianists, for the same reason that great performers should never be called "genius" (if anyone is still called such a thing)—that being reserved for inventors alone. The more of himself the executant exhibits the vulgarer his resolution. But the *dancer*, choreographer or no!

Having just come from Graham's where I watched the heavenly Mae O'Donnell especially, it was still again revealed how personal, how out-and-inwardly primal the medium is, even only to raise an elbow with anguish or laughter behind the shower curtain. Dance is the individual's ultimate expression—a dangerous quality for the instrumentalist. However, it is more difficult tastefully to control one's own mode of expression (the peak of divine creation) than diligently to adjust the renderings of someone else's bright ideas. Everyone could dance with a certain beauty if impossible barriers were smashed, but not everyone could play someone else's music with beauty under the same conditions. So Dance, being more universal, produces necessarily less of the Great. But anyone who dances creates, no matter the formal impediments to his style. Motions of the very young are often overwhelmingly lovely, but their piano playing is never pleasant. When Mae moves she has no instinctive sense of rhythm, no motive of musical line, but on or off beat she's exciting all the same for her body's an electric wave with no brain. Were the same true of an instrumentalist we'd squirm in our seats. And there is only one Martha, but a great number of flawless pianists.

It is amusing to see the kids during class, their lips half-parted in ecstasy, their contractions and releases propelled by desire to rid themselves of what they feel to be "ancestral frustrations." But after class a too-close awareness of their sweet sweat provokes self-consciously coy joking, remindful of scenes in terminals when men-friends greet after long absence with a heart-felt embrace, then start to spar and punch good-naturedly, embarrassed by the previous demonstration unbecoming to the American male.

Salt Lake City, Autumn 1966

Martha Graham I've known, albeit casually, since 1944. Having in that year run away from Curtis Institute to seek Manhattan fortunes as Virgil Thomson's copyist, I earned a few extra bucks a week as accompanist to Martha's classes on lower Fifth Avenue. She hence became my first official employer, for whom I drew out Social Security number 091-22-5307.

Immediately I came to worship with the entourage: as regular worker she showed us the model of Spartan self-denial, scheduling a class even for the hungover blizzardly New Year's dawn; as exceptional artist she showed us how to wander from the beaten track—but only *she* found her way back. Then as now she was America's first female, yet now as then she must solicit subsidy despite that fame. That fame was such that all her girls wore their hair tight in abject adoration, their mouths slightly open, their thighs at skinny angles—but only *she* brought it off. Then like now Martha Graham was of the four most significant influences of any sex, of any domain, of our century. My dream was to compose for her.

But she fired me. Oh, quite nicely, because, as she rightly explained, improvisation was clumsy discipline for young composers. Her unspoken reason was my lack of the pianistic thrust needed to impel collective contractions and releases. Dance accompanists, to be good, must take classes themselves.

Fired me. But today, thanks to that discipline unclumsified by dance class, I've made a music which it seems, so many decades after, she is about to use.

Paris, May 1954

Martha Graham's company is here for the first time. The French who, if only on their deathbeds, do take their free-wheeling birthright Catholicism for granted, do not therefore know how to take the implacable no-nonsense of Martha's Jocastas or Emilys. We had all that with Kurt Jooss, they wrongly clarify (they, who ask with brave discovery if you know the Brahms quintets!). The French are still for toes and fairy-tales, so they have put her down.

Yesterday afternoon, emerging from the Église Saint-Germain into green sunlight, I spotted her at the Deux Magots terrace seated gauntly before a cold demi-tasse and a pile of dry brioches. For a moment we spoke—if indeed speaking is how one communicates with her, if one communicates—and I wandered off, caught again.

Caught by the past when I was as young in New York as now I am in Paris, as enamoured there then of miraculous Frijshian ladies as I am here now of my Marie Laure. And Martha again today, so out of context! How far, on this warm evening, were those nervous mornings during the war's end, of Protestant banging to a count of eight loudly, while in silence

I worried that she choreographed *Dark Meadow* to Chávez' tunes, not mine.

How far, those Grahamesque explications we all understood without understanding, that vague speech on mental landscapes of primeval ritual which did somehow compel the dancers! For we were moved; it worked. The ensuing class was conducted by her near-future but brief spouse, Erick Hawkins, whose humorlessness forced us to take him seriously. We heard his parroted paraphrase of that speech, and somehow were not moved, it didn't work. We went downstairs to the art movie in the same building, while upstairs Martha Hawkins created *Night Journey*.

Tonight I took again her *Night Journey*, dying. Afterward, alive in the wings, I asked Martha (hugely tiny among her wingèd Noguchi's) how long she'd be in town, if we could have iced tea together, or could I show her Versailles. "Yesterday would have been the time for that," she answered, "when you passed by the Deux Magots. From now on I haven't a minute to myself."

•

Salt Lake City, January 1967

For a quarter-century we've socialized at 5-year intervals during parties or backstage, fragmented moments, urgent to me, unrecalled to herself. Then last fall her conductor, Eugene Lester, intoxicated by my *Paris Diary*, felt that Martha and I should meet again, for business now, *tête-à-tête*, on the subject of a collaboration.

She moved toward me across the immensely echoing floor of the rehearsal room. Each step disintegrated the clock until her scarlet mouth was close, uttering the identical phrases of years before, the same words, but which, like those of Nadia Boulanger, took new meanings according to occasion. Random example:

"Oh, Martha," I say, "I'm feeling ghastly—I wish I were dead."

"Ah, when a dancer says 'I've hurt myself,' I answer, yes, it's *we* who hurt ourselves, not the bar."

"The bar? You mean—?"

"Why, Ned." She reeled a bit.

Our indefatigable Spartan reeled. Why not reel, when still famous as before—but who sees her now and not a statue? Can statues create? Sure she reels, alone in the rarefied air, I from rum or sleepiness, her reasons are hers. Looking madly the same, as that silk-voiced repetition, where had I heard it all before? Surely the sickly bittersweet emanations of yesterday's wine can linger through rooms until 3 p.m.

Stock-still for twenty-seven minutes she listened to the tape of *Eleven Studies for Eleven Players*; when it was over she'd all but choreographed it in her head. We shook hands, kissed. It was a deal. Already she had a title, from Saint-John Perse, "The Terrible Frivolity of Hell," and I remembered that, of course, Martha always spoke, ever so softly, in iambic pentameter. . . .

Well, I'll believe it when I see it done, for Bernhardt too was unpredictable.

Autumn advanced with inspired midnight phone calls, cubes tinkling through the wires across our city, Martha's voice accompanying them with tones again I could not understand, but understood; her ballet was evolving.

Will I, here in Utah, see it next month during her Easter vacation New York season, for presumably she works still on it this minute? Meanwhile (though the dream may come true— and Boosey & Hawkes have frozen the option against other choreographers), since the music is both published and recorded other dancers *have* used it before (Valerie Bettis, Norman Walker), but Martha doesn't know. So please don't tell her.

•

February, 1967

Miss Graham in Manhattan has premiered my ballet and called it *Dancing Ground*. Everyone has phoned me here about

its "success," and sent the Clive Barnes clippings. Possibly because the music wasn't written for her, my feeling of high honor
is joined with disinterest. Next week I'll be there and, like
Maldoror, will see for myself.

•

New York, March 1967

The music *was* written for her! Before the fact.

In the past it's been shocking how dancers seem unaware of
what composer they're dancing to. Not Martha's troupe: they
demonstrated how I'd made Eleven Studies in search of an
author. How unright that music was without this sight! How
Helen McGehee's vibrating hops were inevitably correct against
the amorphous trumpet! the group's immobility when my orchestra goes wild! or young John Powell's rhythmic trance behind
the screeching clarinet! Virgil's epigraph was wrong, at least for
now: for now, though they never stop talking but still with
little conversation—meaning they hover over facts while avoiding ideas, except when approaching ideas as though they were
sacred or (what's worse) new—they are so eloquent with their
autoeroticism that speech grows superfluous.

Because she was unliteral, and knew how to design *counter* to
the yet-indispensable music, Martha is my only collaborator
(though she never once asked my advice) to have been right, all
right, turning my disinterest to satisfaction.

And who, to share the satisfaction, did I rashly select to attend
the performance? Of all people, Susan Sontag! By phone I invited her. She said sure, but could she bring a friend. I said
sure. She said wait a minute. Then I overheard her explaining
to someone: "You know, Graham, *Martha* Graham: she dances."
Oh, the shifting generations! Next night we sat in a neat row,
I in my shiny green shirt beside Susan who, with that enigmatic
smile beneath a yard of tresses, offered to my achingly expectant
ears no comment whatsoever.

WHERE IS OUR MUSIC GOING?

•

Time will say nothing but I told you so. . . .
—AUDEN

*Where is music going? Nowhere now. Eventually,
though, it will follow, as it has in the past, wherever
a great monster leads it.*
—NED ROREM

PROLOGUE

More than ever in history, laymen and practitioners today show
concern with the directions music is taking. Where on earth is
it leading us? How should we listen? Could it be that music's
current incomprehensibility, like that of all the arts, indicates
a massive hoax perpetrated by a new society of amateurs im-
puniously calling themselves artists? Are not these amateurs
nevertheless serious in declaring our world so paralyzed by the
increasing victories of matter over mind that nothing makes a
difference? Or could such incomprehensibility signify a final
clarification for the soul as opposed to merely ear or eye, the
courage of the irrational, the last of mimetic subservience, the
first clean air exhaled by creators since the Industrial Revolution
—and everything makes a difference?

Replies depend, as they always have, on how old you are, where you stand, your political sympathies and your overall suppleness; in short, on considerations not directly related to artistic taste.

Some things do appear certain. American artists in the past decade have grown generalized. Unlike Family Doctors who are perishing in ever more specialized arenas, Serious Composers, who once kept company with only each other, are thriving everywhere, because they're working for every medium including that of providing background sounds to look at pictures by. Picture-makers themselves now forsake their easel for mass-producing lithography stones or rubber stamps, for the contagious action of dance, or for the putting together of movies. Heterogeneous, like Paris societies of the past, a 1968 Manhattan gathering comprises graphic artists of conflicting persuasions mingling not only with each other but with musicians of conflicting persuasions, mingling with poets of conflicting persuasions, even scientists who are also violinists, doctors who are also painters, and of course fans (though, unlike in Paris, few creative Men of State show up, art to American politics still being a dirty word). These personalities of conflicting persuasions are nonetheless united in a front against what they name the Establishment, and all seem articulate as can be.

Articulate, yes. Or so I had imagined. Verbal, at least: certainly more so than their pre-war image. For this reason—and because there seemed no longer a clear line between the arts—I had felt that rather than myself composing an essay on the intriguing problem of where music is going, it would be more responsible and anyway original to solicit reactions from a number of acquaintances. "A number of" can never be representative, but you have to start somewhere. My plan was to select and compare opinions from young and old, right and left, from all categories of artist including both the elite and general publics. Like Professor Kinsey I would have access only to Americans, a necessary consideration despite the increasingly homogenized world culture.

Perhaps, thought I, I'll be rebuffed, particularly by the Thoughtful Young who are hesitant to emerge from their paradoxically anarchistic tribes for the likes of me. But friends are friends among the over-thirties, and their aid in this experiment might persuade me to ease up (though why should I?) on my habitual solipsistic manner. Also I realized that in esthetic predictions as in anything worth discussion there are no final answers, only happily mutilated questions. Hopefully these happy mutilations would illustrate just how articulate my colleagues really were.

•

Well, the project landed me at a dead end. For instance, I began on top by visiting an old acquaintance and sometime teacher, Aaron Copland: he, if anyone, would have authoritative opinions as to music's future. At his rambling home near Croton we passed an evening *tête-à-tête* beginning over a succulent platterful of perch filets, and ending with an audition of tapes by one Conlon Nancarrow, an American recluded in Mexico where since the thirties he has composed painstakingly for pianola rolls with flabbergasting results. Meanwhile I attempted to draw out my host on matters prophetic.

But he was not easy to pin down. "I don't get around much anymore," said Aaron Copland, "except to conduct my own concerts. Besides, what with guys like Cage on the one hand and Babbitt on the other, there are so many disparate nuclei, despite the autonomous audience, that it's hard to know just where it will all lead. . . . Yes, we did have rival groups in the Twenties, and for much the same reasons as you now have, but there was nothing that resembled the scene in today's universities. Why, universities used to be hotbeds of conservatism! Education and art were divorced. Suddenly now—and strangely

—schools want to get in on the act. The 'act,' as they see it, is the avant-garde; and the farthest-out composers have quite comfortable jobs. Look at this magazine, for instance."

From a slick pile of new musical periodicals he drew forth *Source*, a luxuriant review edited by Larry Austin at Davis in California. It brimmed with speckled graphs of such intimidating complexity that we both chuckled with defensive amazement. (*Modern Music*, which closed shop in 1946, had been the last magazine devoted to "the cause." But the cause then was multi-leveled. The recent music magazine revival was perpetrated by subsidized groups, each with a specialized axe to grind.)

"The word 'musical' *does* seem now to have less urgency than 'ingenious,'" he went on. "I'd never have guessed this would all come about. Certainly the symphony orchestra situation is not encouraging, as Lenny points out." He was referring to Bernstein's recent question in the *Times* ("Are symphonies a thing of the past? No, since they are still being written. But yes, in the sense that the classical concept of a symphony *is* a thing of the past."). He was referring also to the lack of enthusiasm most "name" conductors have for new music, not so much because it's new as because it's become just too difficult for their allotted rehearsal time; hence the removal from professional concert halls to university gymnasiums as seat of new trends—trends, what's more, now scaled to small ensembles-in-residence backed by Fromm or similar private foundations.

Diplomatically I asked Copland if today's young liked, i.e., took seriously, his most popular repertory works like *Appalachian Spring* or *Quiet City*. (My unspoken intent was to learn whether he was troubled at having been, so to speak, replaced as Leader of American Music—at least for camp-following young turks—by more "complex" composers like Elliott Carter.) "Good lord no," he answered. "Kids no longer can admire a *successful* piece. They want to hear my *Connotations* or *Inscapes* —my serial works. But music that's 'accepted,' that makes money, is automatically suspect. . . . Whom *do* they respect of the recent past? Certainly Varèse more than Ives, precisely because Varèse never *was* accepted by the general public. But even Webern now is almost a 'safe' musician."

And whom, I wondered, did *he* like today, especially among our countrymen? "*Like* is a dubious emotion, assuming it's still a consideration. But I listen willingly, if not always pleasurably, to—hmmm—Xenakis, or, well maybe—Takemitsu. Of course, they're not Americans." Whereupon he mentioned, off the record, a few young U.S.A. composers he sometimes listened to "willingly."

For the most part Aaron Copland did not venture past the first paragraph of a reply to my queries. He had his reasons. Toward midnight, while driving to the train that would deliver me back to Manhattan, he announced the imminent publication of a revision of his 1941 best seller *Our New Music*, now named *The New Music*. Since he had (significantly!) depersonalized his title, I've appropriated his possessive pronoun here for this article, originally called simply *Where Is Music Going?* That's as much as I got out of Copland.

Big shots, I realized, would hesitate at releasing their theories since they have articles of their own to write. (Virgil Thomson frankly declared: "I am less interested in where music is going than in where it has just been," though I'm not sure how he means this.) As for littler shots, I'd planned to interview those from my generation of friends who were either composers themselves or performers or plain music lovers, asking them in particular what music since 1940 they really enjoyed hearing: did they retain today the same energetic curiosity they once felt toward "modern music"? I talked, for example, with Robert Phelps, a quality novelist in his mid-forties, a francophile, a wry and pithy book critic, and husband to the painter, intelligent Rosemarie Beck, herself an amateur violinist. "It was, in fact, exactly twenty years ago," said he, "that I discovered Modern

Music and improvised a little festival in Woodstock—with heroic Henry Cowell (whose name I stole for the letterhead soliciting funds, and who bawled me out but then forgave me and was adorable), with Arthur and Esther Berger, and with vanished Robert Palmer. Now I just settle for what makes me cry—Poulenc, Cole Porter, player piano rolls from my childhood, the *Chansons de Bilitis*."

These words, of course, expressed pure reaction rather than the desired opinion, as did those I received from another friend, John Gruen, composer of a wee but pungent garland of songs, music and art critic turned generalized interviewer, and husband to the painter, gorgeous Jane Wilson, herself an amateur pianist. Like Paul and Jane Bowles in the early forties, this young couple is something of a pace-setter for the sixties, proposing tastes and reflecting moods of the witless but talented peacocks on seesaws. "Where it all will end I wouldn't know," Gruen sighed. "I only wonder where it *can* end. Anyway, the whole scene's exposed in my nice book *The New Bohemia*. But as far as my own music's concerned: what difference—what *sound*—could that possibly make in the total assault of noise that now surrounds us!"

As for my one-time schoolmate, famed pianist Eugene Istomin, when his opinion was sought, he merely went to the phonograph and turned on *Das Lied von der Erde*. "I want beauty," he eventually announced. "Are they, today, composing out of the same *need* as Mahler? Does that need still exist? Do they *hear* what we heard when we were curious kids at Curtis? Do composers want to *communicate*, or merely to distinguish themselves —assuming there's a difference? Myself, I can only perform on the keyboard that which I feel requires my reinterpretation. Yet when the Ford Foundation asked me to commission a composer of my choice, I could think of no one who might write today what Chopin or Rachmaninoff hadn't written better yesterday. So from a kind of perversity I went to Roger Sessions, just because his music was problematic and knotty; not knotty in the pejorative sense, but because, in going against my senses, it went against them *with strength*. And I've always loved problems. Yet though I may never play his piece (it would take six precious months to digest), I'll supervise the rehearsals of whoever *does*. Because I admire Sessions unqualifiedly."

•

Conversation with old friends is often unproblematical, precisely because it is with old friends: the attitudes have become predictable. Like lovers, friends result from involuntary choice, though unlike lovers we accept them because essentially they agree with us. The same holds true for professional colleagues, rivals though they be. Accordingly we acknowledge their conjectures in good faith: we long for them to be right because it makes life easier. But our—and their—good faith is not, by definition, representative (nor can any individual be representative) of an inclusive scene: there is always an enemy camp with a view to be considered. Now, for the individual artist an enemy camp is, of necessity, wrong; artists are artists by virtue of being categorically right, by virtue of their non-magnanimous aristocracy. Most of them do keep their eyes—or, in the case of composers, their ears—open to the tone of the times, if only to avoid what not to do. But inasmuch as they write papers like this one they must momentarily cease being artists and become objective appraisers. Objectivity is not easy, least of all for an artist turned sociologist; and to conduct appraising interviews with the enemy camp takes time, time better employed in making art.

As a result I have decided, after misfiring my initial project, to forget both friends and foes (just as Istomin finally forsook today for yesterday) and, for better or worse, to render this article as a personal *précis*. This I shall now do—I, the musician Ned Rorem—by airing the biases any composer does and must possess from conviction and for armor. These biases will be involuntarily submitted through descriptions of music's shiftings over the recent past, within our mercurial present, and through an uncertain future. About what music was and what it has become I have reached conclusions. About where it resultingly might travel I am as vague as the next one. But however misguided, in prediction lies the vitality of any generation.

WHAT IT WAS

Very different is the outlook of some of our younger masters such as Hindemith, whose renunciation of beauty was in itself a youthfully romantic gesture. . . .

—TOVEY

A work of art does not answer questions, it provokes them; and its essential meaning is in the tension between the contradictory answers.

—LEONARD BERNSTEIN

From just after the last war until 1960 the musical world was split into three categories, each with its own audience and aim of expression. These categories were jazz, experimental, conservative. In that order I'll define them.

•

For lack of a clearer cover-all term, jazz here applies less to the specific Louisiana-Chicago phenomenon than to that music also known as Popular—as distinct from Classical. Classical is equally imprecise ("long hair" would be better) since it really obtains to an historic era and unreally implies a superior intent rather than content. Certainly Popular Music is now history, a history not quickly proven to be less "significant" than Classical Music's. So I shall retain the word jazz, assured that most people understand it as I do.

Pre-war jazz was lavish and immense, exemplified by the Big

Bands of Ellington or Artie Shaw which performed thru-composed, meaning non-improvised, orchestrations. These were arrangements of so-called standards, sumptuous in sound yet rigorous in rhythm, fulfilling the double need for Hollywoodian fantasy and for supporting dance crazes. The arrangements *swung*—with a careful exoticism. Often as not they accompanied vocal "stylists" like Doris Day or Peggy Lee, equally strict and equally glamorous, who crooned sentimental verse in tune with the casual poignance of that epoch's younger generation. The largeness of the period was occasionally counterbalanced by intimate groups-within-the-group (Benny Goodman's Trio, for example), but these were more a quaint indulgence than a necessary antidote. The antidote to the ultimate elephantiasis came with the financial restrictions of World War II. Similarly, a quarter-century earlier, another war had reduced Diaghilevian grandiosities to chamber dimension, hence altering—through economics, not sociology—the whole nature of musical composition.

Probably economy rather than sociology also produced our little post-war groups of Progressive Jazz, although the Brubecks and Mulligans of that decade could hardly be called "uncommitted." Commitment in music, however, is pinpointed through lyrics rather than tunes (could we truly get Weill's "message" without Brecht's texts?), and the new cool movement was wordless. Commitment, as it had been championed in the depressed thirties, was "out" in the fighting forties (except for such harmless horrors as "He's A-1 in the Army and He's A-1 in My Heart"), not to return until our thoughtful sixties. Gone with the war was the oral lament of "At Least You Could Say Hello," the dizzying nonsense of "The Music Goes Round And Round." Gone was the kinetic impulse of Gene Krupa and twenty gold trumpets. And gone too was the Negro aristocracy—the Dukes, Kings, Counts—who had dictated the tone of our first half-century.

Here to stay, or so it seemed, was a breed of swinging Wasp (though Asp would be a less redundant term: Anglo-Saxons are by definition white) bred into "tolerant" milieus, weaned at the conservatory, and launched through clubs that served sodas to an intellectual public. That public, in forgoing dance and song and alcohol, encouraged the growth of a jazz which was improvisational in structure, pseudo-atonal in texture, and eccentric in beat. A few old-time vocalists like Billie Holiday remained stylish, but were heard now, head in hands, as recitalists accompanied by "artists" such as Lester Young. The core of jazz, which like all music had been formed from words which are more than words, was changing from a verbal into an instrumental utterance, an utterance by nature more sophisticated, more artificial, diffuse, "abstract." Instruments, of course, basically are human voices once removed, even tubas, even xylophones, even electronic equipment which, though emulating a bulldozer, inasmuch as it pretends to make music, remains a human expression, a voice. Such a change presupposed more rambling forms; and if an old-timer like Armstrong today still "sings" through his trumpet, the trumpet of Ornette Coleman and his white imitators during the fifties soared higher than human and longer than freedom.

With the admixture of education resulting from a racial integration of jazz performers, it became only logical that experiments be tried. What Gunther Schuller named Third Stream showed attempts at conjoining jazz and classical. The attempts were manifest in the classy, moodily elegant and presumably Schoenbergian but actually Ravelian musings of esoteric combos (like bass flute, vibes, celesta, solo fiddle) as organized by cultured college kids who had sat in on Negro jam sessions during their infancy; in the pitting of a soloist like Maynard Ferguson against a thru-written piece for philharmonic as in Bill Russo's slick Second Symphony; or in the setting of an improvisatory microcosm among a "strict" orchestra as in some of Schuller's own pieces.

The Third Stream flowed with oil and water, never merging but diverging as undirected tributaries that dribbled into limbo by 1960, when jazz finally lost its definition both as a players' art and as a solid compositional medium. It was then—meaning now—that the art of song, for twenty years dormant, was revitalized. Revitalized, not by soloists but by groups; the Andrews Sisters of yore were paralleled most noticeably in the stimulating advent of the Beatles.

•

For lack of a clearer cover-all term, the division called Experimental is a music which in turn may be split into three factions: serial, electronic, chance.

Serial composers are the inheritors of Schoenberg's 12-tone formula as filtered through Webern, then recodified by Boulez in Paris and Babbitt at Princeton. Integral serialism, as the recodification is known, presents the predetermined systemization not only of pitch or tone but of all musical variables: rhythm, dynamics, silence, etc. In opposition to the built-in opulence of jazz—a pleasure in sound for sound—integral serialism was not geared to seduce the senses, having other fish to fry.

Fish is a brain food, never the basic diet of artists from prehistory until World War II. During those millennia the making of music was the making of romance insofar as romance means evasion of reality, or rather, heightened reality, concentration of emotion as against logic, controlled fantasy of self-expression; in short, art, art as expounded by Tolstoy or Freud but never truly defined except through itself. When the atomic age reared its ugly clouds, however, that rising generation which earlier would have been impelled toward art was deflected toward science. Trips to the moon, to inner space, or to death by holocaust, were now practicable voyages, and romance switched from bass clefs to test tubes. Art's function, of course, is not to clear away clouds, nor even to show how clouds could have been cleared. Art mirrors, proposes questions, sometimes alternatives, but never answers. More than ever art now seemed a follower, and those few young talents who inclined toward art necessarily reflected science; their music grew into a demonstration of logic for its own sake rather than for that of "romance." Even mathematicians who, as everyone knows, all relax via musical hobbies, now satisfied their need for mystery via numbers alone.

Serial music, then, was made by brains and performed for brains—when it was performed at all. For performance appeared less and less a prerequisite to the notes (were they still notes?) so exquisitely inscribed as an end in themselves on graph paper, while the joys and terrors of the ear (not to mention the soul) became a negligible, even embarrassing, consideration. Public auditions, such as they were, had mostly left urban concert halls for subsidized campuses. Attraction to such music was nil, since suddenly it could not be heard as we are conditioned to hear—with reference to the past; the organized music of the fifties, although true to that iconoclasm which Thomson names "the tradition of constant change," had evolved by obliterating rather than by incorporating its heritage.

And so by 1960 the purist audience for Integral Serialism—a music more seen than heard—had nearly atrophied from hemophilia: one week's public became next week's performers for an incestuous minority paradoxically claiming some of the decade's healthiest brains.

Meanwhile the more generalized elite of music fans was staring around in a daze. After all, they couldn't listen to Donizetti forever; they wanted to show good will toward modern music, yet shunned those recitals where the only scandal would be tedium. In 1960 it was still low class to admit being bored.

•

Electronic music means the mechanical fabrication of hitherto unheard sonorities and their formal combination. The initial experiments during the war years were most noticeably credited to Frenchman Pierre Schaeffer's *musique concrète,* so-called as distinct from *abstract* music. Schaeffer's new sound fusions and those of Blomdahl, Badings, Krenek and others, resulted from taping "normal" instruments distorted through unusual speeds and eccentric juxtapositions. The psychological outcome was nevertheless, when reduced to lowest terms (disentangled from its novel verbiage), often one of standard concepts made to "sound funny." Certain American works, for instance those of Luening, came off as diatonic ballads heard from under water miles away.

Younger pioneers like our Richard Maxfield and Morton Subotnick, or Cologne's Stockhausen and Venice's Nono, dispensed with instruments altogether and dreamed up strictly electronic collages, collages which by their nature presupposed new structures. Such mechanical essays were, to be sure, not wholly new, deriving as they did from the percussional forays of Varèse and Cowell a half-century earlier. But the total artifice did represent an advance if one assumes, like Stravinsky, that advance means "retrogressing faster." The musician as individual performer had, after all, been disposed of.

By 1960 several universities had set up costly electronic laboratories plus courses in their use. Yet the music seemed still incomplete, not something one could just sit down and listen to. The medium cried out for superimposition on visuals; it succeeded commercially as background for science-fiction movies, non-commercially as accompaniment to modern dance or even to the classical ballet of Balanchine. But it did not yet succeed on a plane alone.

•

If electronic phenomena were of diverse foreign origin, the Music of Chance evolved specifically in America through a single man. John Cage had long been not only a musician but a philosopher of original wit. From his very beginnings he needed for composition to derive not just from its own past, nor even just from the sister arts, but also from points of view and of feeling, from city sounds, the earth itself, mushrooms. He took from—or rather merged with—the vast realm of our world's noise, striving toward an "emancipation of music from its notes."

The emancipation was arrived at through what inevitably became "accidental" operations originating from the *I-Ching*, the Chinese *Book of Changes*. The resultant Chance Music has been more fancily labeled Indeterminate; indeed, *Indeterminacy* is the title of a recorded lecture by Cage. The lecture itself is, if you will, a piece of music, for like so many contemporary musicians Cage has been no less influenced by composers than by writers, not the least of whom is Gertrude Stein. Still, the influence is as much through writers' sound or their look on paper as through their meaning. "I don't give these lectures to surprise people, but out of a need for poetry," explains John Cage. "Poetry is not prose simply because poetry is one way or another formalized. It is not poetry by reason of its content or ambiguity but by reason of allowing musical elements (time, sound) to be introduced into the world of words. Thus, traditionally, information no matter how stuffy (e.g. the sutras and shastras of India) was transmitted in poetry."

His own more "traditional" music may be represented by the do-it-yourself manipulation of radio dials, or the now more-than-notorious *4′ 31″* as executed by a pianist who sits at a closed piano for four minutes and thirty-one seconds: the "music" is the undetermined public reaction (discomfited coughs, bridled approbation) as restricted to this predetermined period. And the public loves it. Not for nothing has Cage's name, second only to Stravinsky's, become a word to international households less than erudite. His extramusical charm is contagious; the question-and-answer sessions following his concerts are more eagerly awaited than the concerts. But if for households he satisfies a need for the all-but-vanished crazy artist (like Callas or Nureyev

satisfy a need for the all-but-vanished temperamental performer),
to the more specialized public he satisfies a solider need.

That need, as I see it, is best explained by the mechanized
West being caught with its pants down. So rapidly has indus-
trialization developed since the war that we've not had time for a
compensating indigenous growth of introspection. Instead we
have reached out for the organized whimsy and wisdom of an
oriental past and superimposed it, come what may, onto our
occidental present. It may be argued that Buddhism's origins
and offshoots had flowered over centuries from a seed native to
foreign ground, a seed unable to survive in our soil. Nevertheless
the plant full grown has been transplanted here where it cur-
rently shades so many aspects of our society. It remains to be
guessed whether the adoption was from superficial desperation
or whether, in fact, now is the time when finally the twain of
East and West shall meet—at least culturally. Surely Japan
since 1945 has advanced philosophically toward us as fast as we
toward her. And as flocks of her dutiful three-year-olds learn the
Suzuki fiddling method while her masterful novelists write of
miniskirted murders, a not-insignificant segment of our composers compose according to the reinterpretation of a religion
which itself was transplanted into Japan from India, where it
had evolved centuries before. Much of this indeterminate music
becomes, in effect, not all that distinguishable from predetermined serial or even electronic works with which, as we shall
see, it has begun to overlap. All the same, its "pure" state had by
1960 outlasted the purity of these other expressions, doubtless
because the *act* of Chance Music, as opposed to the music itself,
fulfilled more urgent impulses.

•

For lack of a clearer cover-all term Conservative composers
are those who persevered (shall we say logically?) according to
European traditions set up in the 1600's. By the late 1930's

those traditions had progressed through us into a readily identifiable American Style. That style, cursorily one of sophisticated diatonic French economy soldered to local hymn tunes, commenced with the practical restrictions of the WPA and reached peak delineation during the war when isolation forced invention. With the armistice the complex chromaticism of Vienna, long latent beneath Hitler and presumably fossilized, was reinvented by the young who deemed it "new." America, seldom secure in matters artistic, again acquiesced, tail between legs, to continental domination. From the ensuing recomplication of chromaticism there crystallized an International Academy exemplified in the "experimental" schools just described.

Yet certain Americans abstained. Roy Harris and William Schuman, say, or younger men like David Diamond and Vincent Persichetti, kept their distance from global vogues, a distance maintained, it would seem, less from spite than from oblivion to the radicalism of the preceding two decades. Through pride and through habit they continued a national tradition.

How to label that tradition? Well, it is far from far-out. Yet Conservative is as inapplicable as Conformist or Conventional. For it is conventional to be In. And since the Ins are far-out, to be far-out is to conform. Call them the Post-Avant-Garde, since in their concern with sound over device they sailed beyond current modes toward a revival of that dubious preoccupation of self-expression.

Self-expression. Ontogenetically as well as phylogenetically, music drags behind the other arts. Writing and painting had mostly withdrawn from obscurantist fashions by 1960. Who knows if a generalized self-expression indeed might not also soon recur as a musical last laugh?

WHAT IT'S BECOME AND
WHERE IT MIGHT GO

If eternity is blue velvet it's a bunch of shit.
—MICHAEL MCCLURE

avant-garde / *those esp. in the arts who create,
produce, or apply, new, original, or experimental
ideas, designs, and techniques; esp: a group that is
extremist or bizarre.*
—WEBSTER'S

Avant-garde is a term so outmoded yet still so over-used as to have grown meaningless. The French vanguard from which the term derives refers, of course, to those military scouts who go on before. It is not arbitrarily that I dated 1960 as the close of our musical world's split; by then the designation avant-garde as applied to "a group that is extremist or bizarre" was de-energized utterly. Perhaps it will regain healthy usage through shifts of sense—like the convolutions of Black, once a patronizing colonial reference that changed to darky, then to colored, to Negro, and finally back to Black, a noun now acceptably noble to both white "liberals" and (presumably) "blacks." Avant-garde has yet to undergo such transition.

By 1960 there no longer existed such disparate groups as Webster names "new, original, or experimental." The "ideas, designs, and techniques" had begun to merge inexorably, wilfully and wistfully. They clustered around a nucleus, at once autonomous and amorphous, which generated white heat, exploded, melted thinly over the planet, then cooled into *one* idea, *one* design, *one* technique. The oneness was collective as to intent, to materials, and to those using the materials. Dissipated or ineffectual were the contradictory architectures which had risen on the cultural plain. Individual verticality seemed less imperative than communal horizontality; since now (to change the metaphor) that the "new" musical tongues were an institution—a sort of Esperanto everywhere spoken—it remained only to interpret them.

The interpretation resulted in dissemination at the expense of creation. Dissemination meant business, not pleasure per se, the business of packaging and distributing a product whose evolution could go no farther on its own. Publication decreased in value since scores were useful mainly to specialized performers whose number, for economic reasons, had also decreased. There were few "live" audiences except for the disk-and-tape industry which expanded by leaps and bounds, ultimately to dictate the taste of the whole musical establishment. Yet if today the ratio of recorded contemporary works stays depressingly small compared to *Scheherazade*, the available proportion is nevertheless fairly representative. Whatever they say, composers desire appreciably larger fan clubs than are provided by select colleges. So, often they spend less time composing than wangling recordings: that is the only way to get their music heard.

Other "kinds" of music too were reorienting themselves, sometimes subconsciously, toward a simplicity antidotal to our mixed-up times, a simplicity nonetheless expensive and thus ideal for records.

Jazz, for instance, in becoming a thoroughly random expression, had reached the end of the line. Most of the devotees changed cars for another trip propelled by the delicious vocal statement of Rock. That statement, in an increasingly wild world, seemed sanely simple, like a troubadour tune—a tune permeated with the special joy, albeit poignant, which had been music's *sine qua non* until the fall of forty-five. Physical reaction was the byword, and we were allowed again to dance and sing. The singing was to verse which, like that of the thirties, dealt with "the times," though the commitment now contained a fantasy of surrealist humor. Back too was Big Band backing, but only as a device made feasible through records. If the Beatles, at least, can afford accompaniment by the London Philharmonic, it is a one-shot deal caught and mass-produced in wax. Many of their sound-effects are borrowed from the experimentalists; yet sound-effects they remain, not integral but arbitrary, like the Zen dice-throwing of Chance composers. Rock's real starting point is with the Community Sing revival dolled up for modern consumption.

Meanwhile, experimental music itself, as defined through its three departments, forsook its avant-gardism-at-any-price and became as scholarly an instruction as 18th-century counterpoint. To electronic equipment was added a system of composition by computers, cheaper and (they say) potentially unlimited. Not only at "Manhattan gatherings" were artists of "conflicting persuasions" united, as stated earlier, but in schools as well. At Juilliard alone, four utterly diverse but world-famous composers now teach side by side, uniting their pupils once a week for exchange concerts. These pupils fuse the trends of their teachers. Their other living idols, if they have any, would be personified more in general practitioners like Foss or Henze than in specialists like Babbitt or Cage (who themselves are no longer all that specialized). Lukas Foss, Berlin bred, reached puberty over here where by 1940 he was already famous for his American style. From that date the length of stylish musical generations (like schools of painting and poetry) telescoped with such acceleration that by the sixties a trend's survival rate was about two weeks. Fair-haired Lukas kept on the bandwagons, leaping from Coplandian open prairies to Stravinskian neo-classicism to post-Gregorian romanticism, to serial, to indeterminate, to jazz, to what he called Pop Art music, and finally to Unsafe. "Composing once meant writing the music I like," he states. "Now it means to me: writing out of a deep concern for new music and for the cause of new music." Which is to say: for publicity. Publicity in itself is no crime; it has even become, as with Warhol, a fine art. But both foes and friends of Foss speculate as to what his "placement" might have been were he less of a generation-hopper. William Flanagan once acumenously suggested that if, a hundred years hence, all of Earth's music had vanished, save that of Foss, historians would still be able to reconstruct a clear picture of our mid-century's fluctuation. Certainly Foss-as-performer has widely serviced the popularizing of abstruse and "significant" modern composers; as to how those men estimate Foss-as-composer remains moot.

Hans Werner Henze, also fortyish and German-born but resident of Rome, seems more fructuous, less compulsive. He was among the first post-war artists to select the best from every plate without risking indigestion from too much of one good thing. "In every phrase you write you can hear your grandfathers," says he, "you can hear Josquin, and Verdi, and Monteverdi, and Mozart. And if you try to deny all this, what you produce will be something inhuman." Like Britain's Britten before him, or our own Lou Harrison, he inclines more toward betterness than toward differentness; his originality lies not in his multilingual ability but in the special grammar built from that ability. Pertinently his talent, like Britten's, "speaks" best through theater pieces—ballet and opera having always been the best focalization for mixed media.

In America the mixing of media other than commoner operatic ones is frequent everywhere. LaMonte Young, for instance, plots pieces (more properly, happenings) expressly to be heard against light projections. Light projections are also of prime function for Alwin Nikolais who prepares his own, who nevertheless calls himself a choreographer, and who composes his own electronic foregrounds. The composite issue resembles a disciplined Electric Circus: well-trained bodies gyrate on languid ropes glazed by whirring rainbows that undulate to spine-splitting squeals. Singularly the evening is neither tiresomely morbid nor gimmickly neurotic, maybe because neurosis and mobidity are impelled by individuality, a quality absent from the young art.

Youth today is collective, no longer out for glory *à la* Beethoven, for "making it" *à la* Podhoretz; it acts through anonymous or through celebrated groups like the Hippies or the Rolling Stones. If chic Andy Warhol still loves his fame, be it said he's pushing forty. But his clan of very young followers is just that, a clan, like Sinatra's. They don't care about masterpieces any more. Communal offerings such as the Chartres Cathedral or *The Chelsea Girls* are not, by definition, masterpieces.

If dance has replaced opera and so-called legitimate plays as the staple of living theater, the "dead" staple of the young art is found at the movies. But curiously, film lacks adventure in mixed-media sound tracks. Very contemporary thinkers in the very contemporary medium of movie making, like Fellini, Antonioni, Godard, with their In tone of alienation and violent "lack of communication," use, when it comes to original scores, either straight jazz, as in *Breathless*, Italianized jazz, as in *Juliet of the Spirits*, or no jazz at all, as in *Red Desert*, which dispensed with any music. The occasional American cinema use of "experimental" sound is predictably restricted to the dream sequence or to drug hallucination.*

---

* Kubrick, in 2001: *A Space Odyssey*, uses three "kinds" of music: 1) For "The Dawn of Man" we hear the noble opening bars of Richard Strauss's *Zarathrustra*, unfamiliar and hence spookily effective—like Cocteau's earlier use of Bach—to ninety-nine out of a hundred. But to the hundredth—or at least to me—the tone poem's previous associations render its present location not noble but ludicrous. (Similarly, twenty years ago, the very young Kenneth Anger, to save money and doubtless banking on the music's unfamiliarity for its effect, garnished his unusual *Fireworks* with an old record of Ernest Schelling's *Victory Ball*, of all pieces! Again then, my previous acquaintance cancelled the score's pseudo-impressionist powers in mixed media.) 2) For the first visions of deep-space travel we hear *in toto* Johann Strauss's *Blue Danube Waltz*, quite familiar and hence campily effective—like Kubrick's earlier use of pop song in *Doctor Strangelove*—to ninety-nine out of a hundred. For the hundredth—at least for me—I couldn't tell why (though why anything, really, in art!) he chose a familiar rather than unfamiliar camp tune, or even camp at all. 3) For ensuing exposition, and for the final infinity-

Thus the Conservatives remain the suitable composers for movie scores because they have taken time to perfect their craft. Like Rock musicians they borrow, if gingerly, from the experimentalists whose inventions they employ as decoration, not as formal points of departure. Conversely, die-hard experimentalists now revert to traditional instrumentation, especially in the more ambitious iron-curtain lands. Take Poland, which, since the war, has given us a Gorecki or a Penderecki who use normal strings to imitate electronic sounds, just as women nowadays tease their real hair to resemble Mod wigs.

If Mod wigs began in England as a style of living, musically they are covered by an old hat. That nation's inherent conservatism is partly accountable to the overwhelming personal dynamics of Benjamin Britten's eclecticism. (Third stream jazz and neo-romantic chromaticism are just starting to take hold there.) And all the young British stem from Britten—even by virtue of denying him—just as Britten stems from Stravinsky, Stravinsky

---

shattering sequence, we hear snatches of works composed years earlier and for other purposes by the Armenian Khachaturian and the Hungarian Ligeti, works already known to that unhappy few who feel such works to be nonaccompanimentory, self-sufficient. Yet the Ligeti especially contains those "current" sonorities (an out-of-focus heavenly choir singing what sounds like *Kyrie*) which, wrongly or rightly, have come to be as identified with science-fiction as Debussy's *La Mer* is with travelogues on Tahiti.

None of the above-mentioned pieces were specifically written for the movie; all were torn from context and superimposed on the finished soundtrack—though not, we suppose, for economic reasons (as in the case of Anger) so much as because Kubrick already knew and just had to have these sounds.

My point is that familiarity does not breed contempt, it just breeds more familiarity. A film about the future cannot, by definition, employ music of the future. Yet the medium's artifice requires music (unless dispensing with music altogether, which amounts to the same thing, since planned silence fulfills the same soldering purpose). The question is, with a movie like this, what *kind* of music? Kubrick, in not running a risk, found no answer. As to what risk he should have run, I have no answer either. But I'm only a composer.

whose retainment of individuality is of itself individual, a last stand.

And France? She has never been musical, despite appearances. Which is to say that, although producing more than her share of great composers plus a number of great performers (performers unable, however, to interpet their composers as well as foreigners do), she has never produced a viable public for these musicians. If the seven lively arts in the countries of our earth can be distinguished as either aural or visual (and they *can*: no fine art except cooking and sex is dedicated to the sense of taste, touch, or smell), the French have always been leaders in the visual. Always, that is, until Rauschenberg acquired the laurel crown in 1961. Which left Paris with little international prestige, her composers having long since emigrated to Germany, of all places.

Soon after the war Germany ironically became a recipient for French "refugees" whose new esthetic, though grudgingly sanctioned, was hardly fostered at home by the old guard. The old guard composers themselves had enough problems getting heard. Led by the dominating genius Boulez, young French musicians took over the willing government-sponsored radio stations and summer festivals of Germany, from where they dictated what soon was to become the International Style. Back home today the newest flock, typical of the Gallic tradition of naughtiness, has already officially dethroned the mentor by composing, I'm told, *Le Tombeau de Boulez*. Boulez himself has now turned into a conductor of classics.

•

Nothing said in these pages is other than common knowledge. If the workings of continental specialists now blur with the workings of American general practitioners, if the devices of English post-impressionists now incorporate Hindu ragas, if the Japanese compose electronically while United States conservatives write symphonies for the expert new Tokyo orchestras; if, in short, the musicians of our ever-shrinking planet are hoeing the tone row together, so indeed are metallurgists and housewives, a parallel which *The Readers Digest* is the first (I mean the last) to draw.

This merging, to summarize, ensued from the cooling-off process following the atomic explosion, an explosion at once scientific and cultural. It tore much of our music from the concert hall (where it had only lasted for a couple of centuries) and put it back in cafés, homes, and public squares. Colleges, for whatever motives, try to keep up with the young art, while the disk industry, with McLuhanesque condescension, provides spot-check renditions of each new style—including Chance Music which self-evidently cannot be recorded and still retain its definition.

Emotion, that poor outmoded concept, has had its ups and downs in music of late. The quote from McClure's *The Beard*, used as epigraph for this section, indicates the new art's fearfully cool viewpoint. Eternity may not be blue velvet; yet despite their media persuasions young artists-as-artists, from The Doors to the Darmstadt cliques, involve our world's finite future in their works. Witness the number of compositions programmatically speaking of Hiroshima or Vietnam. (The best title so far is Lou Harrison's *Peace Piece*.) Whether these intentions come through as heartfelt music, as political cries, or as neither, is open to question.

The open question of what will come is vain but tantalizing. Tantalizing, because it is the primal question of human nature. Vain, because historic events, even history itself, switch focus every year as we funnel faster toward novel philosophies. Certainly we listen now to Mozart in a manner inconceivable to him: he was ignorant of Mascagni and Mildred Bailey who came between to recondition us. And already we hear with different ears the music of only a decade ago. History is a contemporary decision, not what once took place. So forecasts are useless.

Still, is it not fair from all of this to offer some conclusion? As things stand now, music appears in a state of redemption as "an acceptable art." The Wild has turned Establishment. That is a fact. And an establishment such as The National Institute of Arts and Letters, after long catering to experimental coteries, has this year proposed grants to David Del Tredici, Francis Thorne, William Flanagan and myself, the last three being hard-core conservatives if ever there were any! As to the symphony situation, our bigger orchestras—doubtless from survival instinct and from sympathy (or rivalry) with schools taking the bit in their teeth—are now commissioning the more intransigent composers. Of necessity these composers will be coerced into writing more playable (and thus, presumably, more listenable) pieces. They won't think so much about being modern.

Anyway the modern as a concept has probably come to a close. Music's future lies, as always, in discovering and then codifying the present. The future, what's more, automatically takes care of itself. Our problem is Now.

Published Musical Compositions by Ned Rorem

•

SONGS
(Voice and Piano)

Rain in Spring
Lullaby of the Mountain Woman
Echo's Song
Spring
The Nightingale
Visits to Saint Elizabeth's
Three Poems of Paul Goodman:
    What Sparks and Wiry Cries
    Clouds
    For Susan
Three Poems of Demetrios Cape-
    tanakis:
    The Land of Fear
    Abel
    Guilt
Two Poems of Theodore Roethke:
    Orchids
    Waking (No. 2)

Feed My Sheep
Four Poems of Tennyson:
    Now Sleeps the Crimson Petal
    Ask Me No More
    Far, Far Away
    The Sleeping Palace
To You
Epitaph
A Christmas Carol
The Lordly Hudson
Spring and Fall
Little Elegy
On a Singing Girl
Philomel
What If Some Little Pain
Alleluia
Requiem
The Silver Swan

The Resurrection
An Angel Speaks to the Shepherds
To Poulenc
The Mild Mother
The Tulip Tree
The Midnight Sun
A Song of David
Psalm of Praise
Jack L'Éventreur
Poem for F
Boy with a Baseball Glove
Song of Chaucer
Root Cellar
I am Rose

Snake
Night Crow
The Lord's Prayer
As Adam Early in the Morning
Memory
Such Beauty as Hurts to Behold
The Waking
O You Whom I Often and Silently
    Love
My Papa's Waltz
Sally's Smile
Youth, Day, Old Age, and Night
Early in the Morning
See How They Love Me

Pippa's Song
In a Gondola
Song For a Girl
Rondelay
Credil Song
To a Young Girl Going into Town

} Also available as
*Six Songs for
Very High Voice
and Small Orchestra*

SONG CYCLES

1946   Seven Little Prayers (Paul Goodman)
1947   Three Blues of Paul Goodman
1948   Three Incantations for a Marionette Play (Boultenhouse)
1949   Penny Arcade (6 poems by Harold Norse)
1950   Flight for Heaven (10 poems by Herrick, for bass-baritone)
1951   Another Sleep (3 prose-poems by Julien Green, for bass-baritone)
1951   To a Young Girl (6 poems by Yeats, for bass-baritone)
1951   Cycle of Holy Songs (4 Psalms)
1951   From an Unknown Past (7 choruses in reduction for low voice and piano)
1953   Eclogues (6 poems by Fletcher)
1953   Poèmes pour la Paix (6 poems in French)

1953–54 Four Dialogues (Frank O'Hara) with Two Pianos
1954 Anacreontiche (4 poems by Vitorelli, in Italian)
1961 King Midas (10 poems by Howard Moss, for 2 singers)
1963 Three Poems of Tennyson
1963 Poems of Love and the Rain (17 songs on American poets, for mezzo-soprano)
1964 Two Poems of Plato (in Greek)
1966 Hearing (7 poems by Kenneth Koch, for medium voice)
1968 Some Trees (poems by John Ashbery, for three singers)

CHORUS

Unaccompanied
1946 Four Madrigals (SATB)
1951 From an Unknown Past (Seven Songs: SATB)
1955 Five Prayers for the Young (SSA or TTB)
1955 Gentle Visitations (SSA or TTB)
1955 A Far Island (SSA or TTB)
1955 Three Hymn-Anthems (SATB):
  Sing My Soul
  All Glorious God
  Christ the Lord Is Ris'n
1956 I Feel Death (TTB)
1961 Virelai (SATB)
1967 Hymn: Love Divine, All Loves Excelling (SATB)
With Organ (SATB unless otherwise noted)
1943 The Seventieth Psalm
1953 The Corinthians
1959 Miracles of Christmas
1960 Prayers & Responses
1966 Truth in the Night Season (Psalm 92)
1966 Votive Mass of the Holy Spirit (unison chorus)
1966 He Shall Rule from Sea to Sea
With Strings
1947 A Sermon on Miracles (unison chorus)
1962 Two Psalms and a Proverb
With Orchestra
1943 The Seventieth Psalm (winds and brass)

1955–56 The Poets' Requiem (6-part chorus, soprano solo, full orchestra)
1962 The Ascension (winds, brass, timpani)
1964 Laudemus Tempus Actum (full orchestra)
1966 Paris Journal (chamber orchestra)

VOICE AND ORCHESTRA

1950 Six Irish Poems (mezzo voice)
1954 Six Songs for High Voice and Orchestra (also available in piano reduction)
1966 Sun (for female voice and large orchestra)

VOICE AND STRING-QUARTET

1947 Mourning Scene

OPERA

A CHILDHOOD MIRACLE — 1952
Libretto by Elliott Stein
6 singers, 13 instruments
35 minutes
THE ROBBERS — 1956
Libretto by the composer
3 male voices, 13 instruments
29 minutes
LAST DAY — 1959
Libretto by Jay Harrison
1 baritone and 6 instruments
6 minutes
THE ANNIVERSARY — 1961 (incomplete)
Libretto by Jascha Kessler
3 principals, full chorus and orchestra
Two acts, two hours

MISS JULIE — 1964
Libretto by Kenward Elmslie (after Strindberg)
3 principals, full chorus and orchestra
Two acts, two hours

PIANO

1948	First Sonata
1948	Toccata
1949	A Quiet Afternoon (9 easy pieces)
1949	Barcarolles
1950	Second Sonata
1950	Concerto No. 2
1954	Third Sonata
1955	Burlesque
1958	Slow Waltz
1968	Spiders for keyboard (harpsichord)

TWO PIANOS

1950	Sicilienne

TWO VOICES AND TWO PIANOS

1953–54	Four Dialogues for tenor, soprano, and two pianos (20 minutes)

FOUR HANDS (ONE PIANO)

1967	A Birthday Suite

ORGAN

1949	Pastorale

CHAMBER

1946   Concertino da Camera (harpsichord and 7 instruments)
1948   Mountain Song (flute and piano)
1949   Violin Sonata (in four scenes)
1950   String Quartet No. 2 (4 movements)
1950   Lento for Strings
1957   Sinfonia for 15 Wind Instruments (and optional percussion)
1958   Pilgrims, for Strings
1959   Eleven Studies for Eleven Players
1960   Trio for Flute, Cello, and Piano
1961   Ideas for Easy Orchestra
1964   Lovers (Narrative in 10 Scenes) for harpsichord, oboe, cello, & percussion
1966   Water Music (Violin and Clarinet Solos, with small orchestra)

ORCHESTRA

1950   First Symphony (24 minutes)
1950   Lento for Strings
1950   Second Piano Concerto
1953   Design for Orchestra
1955   Second Symphony (18 minutes)
1957   Third Symphony (5 movements, 23 minutes)
1958   Eagles
1961   Ideas (8 short and easy pieces)
1963   Lions
            Transcription: six songs of Chopin (1959)
            See also categories for Voice & Orchestra, and Chamber:
                        Eleven Studies
                        Six High Songs
                        Six Irish Poems
                        Pilgrims for Strings
                        Sun, for voice and orch.
                        Water Music

THEATER

PAGEANT
1946   *That We May Live* (2 hours), with Milton Robertson
PUPPET SHOWS
1947   *At Noon upon Two* (Charles Henri Ford)
1947   *Fire Boy* (Boultenhouse), with John Myers
MUSICAL COMEDY
1958   The Ticklish Acrobat (Kenward Elmslie)
INCIDENTAL MUSIC
1948   *Hippolytus* (Euripides), with Muriel Smith and Donald Buka (Anta Theater)
1948   *Dusk* (Paul Goodman), Picastor's Poets' Theater
1949   *Cock-A-Doodle* (Iris Tree), with Charlton Heston and Darren McGavin (Anta Theater)
1950   *Il n'y a plus rien à vivre* (Mauroc), Paris Theater
1955   *The Young Disciple* (Goodman), The Living Theater (Judith Malina and Julian Beck)
1958   *Suddenly Last Summer* (Tennessee Williams), with Anne Meacham (Herbert Machiz, director; John C. Wilson, producer)
1959   *The Cave at Machpellah* (Goodman), at the Living Theater
1960   *Motel*, with Siobhan McKenna (Machiz, director)
1962   *Caligula* (Camus), Albright Theater, Buffalo
1963   *The Lady of the Camellias*, with Susan Strasberg (Zeffirelli, director)
1963   *The Emperor* (Pirandello), Siletti in Cincinnati
        Color of Darkness (James Purdy) Margaret Barker, director
1964   *The Milk Train Doesn't Stop Here Anymore* (Williams), with Tallulah Bankhead and Tab Hunter (Tony Richardson, director)

BALLET

1948   Death of the Black Knight (with Paul Goodman)
1951   Mélos (Marie Laure)
1951   Ballet for Jerry

1952	Dorian Gray (with Jean Marais)	
1959	Early Voyagers (Valerie Bettis)	
1963	Eleven by Eleven (Norman Walker)	
1964	Antics for Acrobats (J. Marks)	(all based on *Eleven Studies*)
1965	Excursions (M. Gordon)	
1966	Lovers (Glen Tetley)	
1967	Sculptures (Ririe and Woodbury)	
1967	Dancing Ground (Martha Graham)	

The music on the above list is represented by the following publishers: Boosey & Hawkes, C. F. Peters Inc., E.C. Schirmer, Southern Music, Elkan-Vogel, Hargail, Novello, H.W. Gray, Presser, Mercury Music Corporation, and Associated Music Publishers.

Index of People